The Lunar Living Journal

The Lunar Living Journal

*A guided moon journal to help you
find joy, clarity and purpose*

KIRSTY GALLAGHER

First published in Great Britain in 2021 by Yellow Kite
An Imprint of Hodder & Stoughton
An Hachette UK company

4

Copyright © Kirsty Gallagher 2021

Illustrations by The Colour Study © Hodder & Stoughton 2021

The right of Kirsty Gallagher to be identified as the Author
of the Work has been asserted by her in accordance with
the Copyright, Designs and Patents Act 1988.

A CIP catalogue record for this title is available from the British Library

Hardback ISBN 978 1 529 36022 6

Typeset in Celeste by Hewer Text UK Ltd, Edinburgh
Printed and bound in Great Britain by Clays Ltd, Elcograf S.p.A.

Hodder & Stoughton policy is to use papers that are natural, renewable
and recyclable products and made from wood grown in sustainable
forests. The logging and manufacturing processes are expected to
conform to the environmental regulations of the country of origin.

Yellow Kite
Hodder & Stoughton Ltd
Carmelite House
50 Victoria Embankment
London EC4Y 0DZ

www.yellowkitebooks.co.uk

Contents

Introduction

Welcome to *The Lunar Living Journal* – a journey to your heart and soul through the magic of the moon.

After the huge success of my debut *Sunday Times* bestselling book, *Lunar Living: Working with the magic of the moon cycles*, many of you requested a moon journal. And here it is.

Once more, I have poured my very essence into these pages – and, of course all of the moon magic – so that you can connect more deeply with a lunar-inspired existence to bring about awakening and transformation in your life, and most of all, know and love yourself like never before.

You may notice that I refer to the moon throughout this journal as she/her. This is because the moon is seen as the powerful feminine energy of the universe. After living alongside her for 13 years, we are on very familiar terms, and I hope that once you have completed this journal, you will get to know her just as well.

The journal can be used as a standalone, but I would suggest that you embark on this journey with *Lunar Living* as your companion, to help you understand the ebb and flow of the moon and the effects that she has on us, as well as her phases and deeper insights into the moon in each zodiac sign.

WHY I WROTE *THE LUNAR LIVING JOURNAL*

I have journaled for as long as I can remember. For me, it's part of a daily ritual. It helps me to make sense of the jumble of thoughts and emotions that come and go within me; it's a place I can pour out my heart and hold space for myself to heal, create and connect inward. We so often bottle up our feelings and hold things in, especially when it comes to our innermost emotions, fears, doubts and beliefs – those things we would rather no one else knew. But when we do this, we get blocked; we disconnect, deny and turn away from ourselves. Journaling is a safe space to honour all that you are feeling and give yourself permission to be who you need to be in that moment. It helps you to understand, know, accept, heal and love yourself on an incredibly deep level.

I love to journal first thing in the morning, before the world has woken up, before the day has even begun. It feels like I'm starting the day with a clean slate and helps me to set a focus and intention for my day, so I can move through the day already aligned with myself and my inner world. I also journal in the evenings, especially during periods of transition, and when I'm navigating tricky times in my life. This allows me to get all of my thoughts and emotions out on paper before I go to sleep, rather than having them run around inside my head, keeping me awake. Putting pen to paper at night helps me to process and release the day, which is very therapeutic.

To be honest though, my journal is never far away from me, and I will often let the words flow out in a stream of consciousness when my mind is overwhelmed by thoughts or I am overcome by emotions, struggling to make sense of things. Through journaling, I often find clarity, answers and the real truth of what is going on for me. My journal is a place where I can be my most honest, raw and authentic self and get to know myself in a truly powerful and intimate way. In this frantic, high-speed digital world, there is nothing more cathartic than taking a moment for yourself and putting pen to paper.

My intention with this journal is to help you find a deeper connection to both the power in the sky, and also within you, so that rather than just reading my words, you can relate to your own musings and begin to develop a more personal relationship with the moon and her guidance and wisdom.

In astrology, the moon represents your inner world: your emotions and dreams, who you are when no one else is around. Your moon sign in your birth chart shows you what you need in life to feel safe and secure, and what you need to nurture and nourish in your world in order to feel at home in yourself, whole and complete (you can find out your moon sign by heading to my website www.kirstygallagher.com). Getting to know your moon sign and journaling with the moon will help you to know and understand yourself in a profound way.

WHAT'S IN THE JOURNAL?

This journal is split into two parts. In Part 1, you'll find all you need to know to begin your journaling journey. This section will cover how to use the moon phases to journal and what you should be focusing on during each phase. It includes a detailed breakdown of the dark, new, first-quarter, full and last-quarter moon phases, with information about what you need to be focusing on in each phase. There are also bonus chapters on how to create a more magical ritual around your journaling experience and the art of setting intentions. Part 2 is the journal itself and is divided into new- and full-moon reflections, with a section for the new and full moons in each of the 12 zodiac signs, taking you through an entire lunar year. There is also an extra chapter (Chapter 6), as each year there will be 13 new or full moons; this section is here for you to weave your own moon magic with this extra moon.

To find out all the dates of the new, first-quarter, full and last-quarter moons, visit www.kirstygallagher.com.

HOW THIS MOON JOURNAL WILL HELP YOU

Journaling with the moon helps to develop a more personal relationship with yourself and your inner psyche using the wisdom and guidance of the moon to access your intuition and connect you back to yourself and who you truly are.

Just as the moon turns the tides of the earth, she exerts the same gravitational pull on the watery inner world of our emotions and inner needs, dreams and desires, highlighting for us where we are out of alignment, not taking care of our own needs or giving away too much of ourselves, or where we are pretending or hiding or not showing up for ourselves.

As the moon helps you to tune into these emotional tides and pulls to the surface all you need to be made aware of, journaling in alignment with her will help you to rediscover your inner world, using your emotions as signposts for what in your life needs your attention or has to change. You'll learn to tune into the call of your dreams and desires, the voice of your intuition and connect to something deeper within yourself: an inner strength and wisdom that will guide your way forward.

Sitting down with yourself each new and full moon will also help to keep you accountable and in control of your own life. So often, we allow ourselves to just drift, perhaps sometimes wishing things were different, but never taking control and making changes. We may make new year's resolutions or set some goals on our birthdays, but rarely do we undertake the consistent work of transformation. This journal will revolutionise all that.

Filling these pages will help you to follow your dreams and stay in alignment with the direction you want to head in. Month by month, moon by moon, you will check in with yourself and where you currently are. And from there, set intentions, work towards achieving them and releasing whatever has stood in the way, reflecting, reviewing, refocusing, realigning and staying in a constant state of connection and flow in your life. Put simply, this journal will be a trusted confidante, bringing you back home to yourself.

The moon is our soul, our inner world, the place of our dreams. Use the connection you make with her, along with this journal, to help you forge a deeper connection with you – meeting yourself, once again, in the portal of your heart, under the moon.

With all the lunar love and moon magic,

Kirsty

A new you is arising
from the ashes
of your past.

Part 1:

Where to Begin

CHAPTER 1

How to Use This Journal

THE JOURNAL HAS been broken down into new-moon and full-moon reflections in each zodiac sign, taking you on a full lunar journey through the year. The zodiac signs will help you to reflect and focus on different areas of your life as the moon brings the various influences, lessons and the magic of each sign into the spotlight for you to work with. There are fire signs (Aries, Leo and Sagittarius), earth signs (Taurus, Virgo and Capricorn), air signs (Gemini, Libra and Aquarius) and water signs (Cancer, Scorpio and Pisces) and each brings about different energies (see box on page 5).

Within each section there is also a waxing-first-quarter (under the new moon) and waning-last-quarter (under the full moon) reflection moment. These are the halfway points of the waxing and waning cycles of the moon and they provide a wonderful time for a check-in to keep you accountable and make sure that you are still travelling on the path towards your dreams. I have also included a dark-moon reflection moment under the new-moon section, as this is the ending that creates a new beginning and is the most insightful and deeply healing part of the lunar cycle.

Use these moments of refection to allow the moon to reveal your soul and inner wisdom to you. See this lunar-inspired check-in time as an appointment with yourself – a time set aside to dedicate to your growth and getting to know yourself like never before. As you do this work, you'll see recurring patterns, self-doubts and all the ways in which you hold yourself back and keep yourself small, and that is when you can begin the restorative work of healing and moving beyond these. You'll also begin to witness and trust in your own abilities, believe in your greatness, become your most authentic self, step into your power and start to realise what you want from life and who you are here to be.

In each chapter there are journal prompts to help bring you closer to your essence, to what is stirring and trying to make itself known, helping you to tune in and listen to your intuition and to live life from the guidance of your heart and wisdom of your psyche. There is also a section for you to write your own insights, feelings, guidance and wisdom from the moon. Use this to journal about your own experiences with the energies of this particular moon and what this moon has shown and taught you. If you need more space to write down your thoughts, feel free to journal in a notepad alongside this book. It really helps to create sacred time and space around your journaling, to make it a ritual, more on this in Chapter 2.

Your journey through the zodiac signs

The journal will take you on a full lunar journey through the year. There are 12 signs of the zodiac, broken down into elements and modalities, each sign being represented by a symbol and bringing a unique energy and influence, helping you to reflect on different areas of your life as the moon brings the various influences, lessons and magic of each zodiac sign into focus for you to work with.

Modalities

The modalities are cardinal, fixed and mutable. The cardinal signs begin each season, and so are the leaders and creators – they initiate things. The fixed signs help to get things done and bring a sense of stability. The mutable signs bring endings, transition and change.

Elements

The elements are fire, earth, air and water. The fire signs tend to bring a lot of motivation and passionate drive to get things done; the earth signs ground you, bringing clarity and focus; the air signs produce change and action; and the water signs put you more in touch with your emotions and intuition.

WHERE WILL THIS JOURNAL TAKE YOU?

This journal will guide you through the dark-, new-, first-quarter-, full- and last-quarter-moon phases, using the energy of each to deepen your journaling experience.

New-moon reflections

Dark-moon reflections: the dark moon is also known as the waning crescent or balsamic moon. These few days just before the new moon, when the moon has waned so far in the sky she is barely visible, are some of the most potent and insightful days of the lunar cycle.

It is during the days of the dark moon that the moon pulls your awareness deep within, down into your inner world. The lowest energy point of the lunar cycle, it's often the most emotional too. It's essential that you tune in and listen to what you are being shown during the dark moon and use this time to journal on who and what you feel the most emotional about. This is your inner guidance system trying to show you the ways in which you are out of alignment in your life. Emotions come along as signposts to point to the areas of your life that need your love, care and attention over the coming lunar cycle. Use this journaling time to get all your emotions on to paper, so that you can see where you currently are.

Using what you learn in the emotional days of the dark moon helps you to set your new-moon intentions.

New-moon soul reflections: the new moon is the day the moon catches up with the sun and both are aligned in the same zodiac sign in the sky. It is the time for starting over, setting intentions and deciding what you want to create over the next lunar month.

The soul-reflection questions will help you to delve deep into where you currently are in your life. They will help to bring you back into alignment with where you want to go and who you want to be, allowing you to continually move forward in your life.

New-moon intention setting: from your new-moon soul reflections, decide on what your intentions will be for the following lunar cycle, and perhaps beyond. These intentions will help keep you focused and on track towards how you want to invest your energies and what you want to create and achieve in your life. Any time you find yourself with a decision to make, unsure about a choice that needs to be made or a little lost or disheartened, look back at these intentions. Ask yourself, 'Will this take me closer to or further from my new-moon intentions?'. See them as your true north, guiding you towards your dreams.

As the moon waxes and grows bigger in the sky each night, this is the time to do all you can to achieve your new-moon intentions, goals and dreams. Show up, say yes, go after all you desire and use the growing light and illumination of the moon to help guide the way.

First-quarter reflections: the first-quarter moon comes around a week after the new moon. This is the halfway point of the waxing part of the lunar cycle: the moon is halfway between new and full, and if you look up in the sky, you'll see a perfect half-moon shining there.

The first-quarter moon brings with it an influx of vitality, inspiration, motivation and a sense that everything is starting to come together. This is the time of the lunar cycle to be fully in the flow of life, and notice all the opportunities, synchronicities and signs around you. Say yes to it all and follow the lead of the growing light and energy of the moon. Under the first-quarter reflection, journal around where you are being guided and the exciting things that are showing up for you in your life. What has taken you closer to your new-moon intentions and dreams?

You may also notice around the first-quarter moon that doubts start to creep in, and you fall into self-sabotage or give in to old fears around not being good enough or deserving of what you desire. Journal on these too, as you will begin to notice a theme emerging around what always seems to prevent you from fully committing to and following your dreams. You will gain so much self-awareness through these insights.

Full-moon reflections

Full-moon soul reflections: the full moon is the day the moon and sun once more align in the sky, but this time on opposite sides of the earth.

This is the time to celebrate what you have achieved through the cycle so far and what has come to completion, and to begin to get clear on what stood in the way or held you back and what needs releasing in the waning part of the lunar cycle. The soul-reflection questions will help you to see all this.

Full-moon celebration: one thing we don't do enough as humans is to celebrate *ourselves*. We are quick to see our own faults or where we could have done better, but celebrating ourselves is so powerful and actually helps us begin to believe in our own magic. Use these celebration moments to look back at the last new moon; journal on what you achieved or did well, steps you took towards something or times when you were brave and simply showed up. These insights will help you to see and believe in how capable you are of following the call of your heart and achieving your dreams.

Full-moon releasing: using your full-moon soul reflections, decide what you now need to work on letting go of in the next half of the lunar cycle. Look back to your first-quarter reflections: where did you let fears, self-sabotage, procrastination or self-doubt get in the way of going after what you wanted? What has prevented you from achieving what you set out to accomplish on the new moon?

Get very clear here on what you need to release, let go of and end. This could be your own stories, beliefs, doubts and fears, or people, situations, relationships, resentments, habits – anything and everything that has held you back, keeping you stuck and small.

As the moon wanes and becomes smaller in the sky each night, use her waning light and energy to heal, surrender, release and let go.

Last-quarter reflections: the last-quarter moon comes around a week after the full moon. It is the halfway point of the waning part of the lunar cycle, when the moon is halfway between full and new, and if you look up in the sky, you'll once more see a perfect half-moon shining there.

The last-quarter moon brings a sense of true release and a need and desire to wrap things up, close them off and let go, making space for new beginnings.

Journal on what you have learned and experienced so far through the lunar cycle and what you are ready to heal and release. What no longer serves you, and what do you want to close, complete and shed from your life, not taking it into the next lunar cycle with you?

You will also notice that I talk of the traditional and astrological years throughout this journal, as well as the solstices and equinoxes.

The traditional year is the calendar year as we know it, running from 1 January to 31 December. The astrological year begins as the sun moves into Aries, usually around 21 March, marking the spring equinox and the beginning of spring. This is then followed by the summer solstice, as the sun moves into Cancer, around 21 June, the autumn equinox as the sun moves into Libra, around 23 September and the winter solstice as the sun moves into Capricorn, around 22 December.

To my southern-hemisphere readers: as you know, your seasons will be reversed, so please take this into account when using this journal and adapt as needed.

Moon reflections made easy

🌟 **Dark moon:** the time for delving deep into your emotions and tuning in to your intuition and inner guidance. Journal on who and what you are feeling the most emotional about and what your emotions seem to be signposting you towards to get an idea of what needs your attention during the following lunar cycle.

🌟 **New moon:** the time for deciding what you want to create in the next lunar cycle and setting your intentions. Use the new-moon reflections to get clear on this, and from here set your new-moon intentions to give you clarity, focus and dreams to work towards through the waxing part of the lunar cycle.

🌟 **First-quarter moon:** the halfway mark between the new and full moon. Use this to reflect on how much you are working towards or being pulled away from your intentions and dreams. Journal on what is working well and falling into place, and what seems to be difficult or any doubts and fears that are surfacing.

★ **Full moon:** the time for completion, celebration and release. Use the full-moon reflections to get clear on what you've achieved and what's stood in the way. Use these insights to celebrate your wins and set your releasing intentions for the waning part of the lunar cycle.

★ **Last-quarter moon:** the halfway mark between the full and new moon. Use this to reflect on what needs to be released from your life and any healing work that you need to do. Journal on what you have learned about yourself so far in the cycle: what always seems to hold you back, and what isn't working for you in your life and needs to be changed or let go of.

CHAPTER 2

Create a Magical Journaling Ritual

IT REALLY HELPS to bring more power and magic to your journaling when you make it into a ritual. A ritual can make something more sacred, symbolic and significant. Below I have suggested ways that you can bring more meaning to your journaling experience. As you gain more confidence, feel free to adapt and create your own rituals to bring lunar living to life for you.

HOW TO HAVE A MAGICAL JOURNALING EXPERIENCE

🌟 Set some time aside for your journaling, switch off your phone and make sure that you won't be disturbed while you are doing it.

* Begin by cleansing the space that you are going to journal in. Also known as smudging, this helps to clear and purify the energy of the room and signifies the start of your ritual. Light some sage or Palo Santo, blow out the flame and gently waft the smoke around the edges of the room, paying attention to corners and doorways. You can also smudge your journal and any other sacred objects like candles or crystals – and even yourself, if you feel your energy needs some clearing! You can leave a window slightly open to save setting off fire alarms and to keep the energy flowing.

* Light a candle or incense or put some calming oils, such as patchouli, lavender or bergamot in an aroma diffuser.

* Make a soothing drink. Cacao is wonderful for opening and tuning into your heart. Or you may prefer chamomile or lavender tea to bring a sense of calm. There are lots of companies offering tea blends for a variety of different things, from relaxation and purification, to dream teas and love teas. Or you can enjoy creating and blending your own by buying loose herbs and dried flowers to suit your specific needs at each moon.

* If you have crystals, gather them together – setting intentions with crystals brings even more power. You may surround your journaling space with your favourite crystals or hold one or two of them as you tune into the energy of the moon, meditate and set your

intentions. Moonstone is always a wonderful crystal to begin to work with the energy of the moon.

✹ Maybe take your journal out into nature – especially under a full moon, it can feel so potent to journal in your garden or a park. You can even gather with friends to create a moon circle where you share your intentions, hopes and dreams to bring them to life and give them more power.

✹ Pick a time in the day when you feel most reflective – perhaps in the morning before you've started your day or when you've just got into bed, ready for a good night's sleep.

✹ Practise a short meditation before you start writing to ground and connect you to the energies of the moon:

  ✴ Close your eyes and take a few long, slow, deep breaths, allowing yourself to relax and become present.

  ✴ Visualise the moon in the sky above you. (On a full moon this will be easy, as she will be full and bright; on a new moon she will not be visible in the sky, but her energies are just as strong.)

  ✴ Begin to connect to the energies of this particular moon. Feel as though magical beams of moonlight are shimmering down all around you.

  ✴ Start to breathe this moon energy in with each breath and feel it filling every cell of your body. Feel the moon's wisdom and guidance fill your whole body, your heart, mind and soul.

* Take some time to simply feel and breathe, just noticing what comes to you under the energies of the moon. If you need any answers or guidance from the moon, you can ask for them and notice what comes to you.
* When you feel ready, open your eyes and begin to journal.

CHAPTER 3

The Art of Setting Intentions

THROUGHOUT THIS JOURNAL, you will hear me speak a lot about intentions. I will also be asking you to set your own intentions under each new moon. But what does this mean?

INTENTIONS – WHAT ARE THEY?

To me, an intention is what gives your life direction, meaning and purpose. Imagine setting out on a journey with no map or any idea of where you were headed. You would so easily be set off track or led along by other people's journeys and plans. You'd maybe stay in a place way longer than you were meant to, or become stuck somewhere you weren't supposed to be at all, simply not knowing where to go next or how. This is what happens to us in life. Life is a journey, and unless we take conscious control over its direction, we will always be powerless, wandering aimlessly through it.

This aimless wandering makes it all too easy to blame everyone and everything else around us for how life is turning out: it's their fault it's like this, or I feel like this because they did that (insert your own excuse). We wait for something outside of us to change before we can be happy, move on, live the life we want. But in truth, we need to stop thinking of ourselves as victims. Our lives are within our control and the direction they take is up to us. We need to accept where we are, take responsibility for how we got here and then take back the authority to do what's necessary.

This is what intentions do for you. They help you to stay in control. They give you something to aim towards, a destination to head for. Your intention becomes a guiding force in your life that helps to align your feelings, thoughts, values, actions, attitude, decisions and the way you show up in life every day. In all moments of worry, fear or indecision, you can ask, 'Does this take me closer to or further from my intention?' You begin to live more purposefully, and life takes on much more meaning as you consciously take part in your own life and live, rather than just existing and feeling as though life is out of your control – something that just happens to you. I usually suggest working with no more than three intentions at once, otherwise you risk diluting the amount of energy and focus you give to each one.

Setting intentions with the moon is even more valuable, as you have the power in the skies guiding you too. For centuries, our ancestors used the moon to guide their journeys, and now you get to do the same. Working with your intentions in this lunar way helps you not only to work towards achieving your intentions, but also to release what stands in the way. Lunar cycle by lunar cycle, you set your intentions with the new moon, allowing the growing light and energy of the waxing moon to guide you towards making them a reality. The full moon brings a moment of gratitude and celebration where you get to appreciate all of the changes you are making, and also an honest reflection of what stood in the way and needs work and attention in the waning cycle. The waning lunar cycle, in turn, helps you to let go of everything that kept you out of alignment with your intentions.

The moon also keeps you accountable, so that your intentions are not just some ideal, long dreamed of but never followed or achieved. They are tangible and real. Some will happen quickly, while others may take longer to bring to life, but you are constantly checking in with where you are and reminding yourself of your intentions, to make sure that you stay in alignment with the direction in which you want your life to go.

Intentions and goals – how are they different?

A goal is something external and future-based, linked to an achievement or end result. One may say that goals help you to get something specific completed – perhaps a promotion, buying a house or saving a certain amount of money. Goals are about 'doing', whereas an intention is about 'being'. It comes from your heart and is about an inner desire to change.

It happens more in the present moment and is something that you embody; it is a way that you live your life, and, as such, it takes you towards what you want to create in it.

I feel it's essential to set both intentions and goals, and so I encourage you to establish goals around a new moon too, especially if there are clear, specific things you want in your life with a time frame – say, to run a marathon, for example. Here, the goal would be to run a marathon, while the intention would be to feel fit and healthy and strong in your body and mind. Or, in the context of a promotion, the goal would be to get the promotion, while the intention would be to feel valued and appreciated and get what you deserve for the good job that you do. The two work really powerfully together, with the goal being the specific outcome you desire and the intention being the energy behind getting you there: the 'why' you want what you want, and the 'how' you will live and show up and feel on the journey towards realising it.

HOW TO SET INTENTIONS

With the dark-moon check-in and new-moon soul-reflection questions, this journal will help you to get really clear on what you want to create in your life and, from there, to set intentions to get you there. As we've learned, the dark-moon phase pulls you deep into your inner world, so that you get the opportunity to see where you currently are, and what needs your attention – what in your life needs you to put some intention behind it. Then the new moon brings you the blank slate that you need to begin again and work towards the changes you wish to create in your life for the better.

Intention setting made easy

1. From this place of knowing what you *don't* want, what *do* you want? How would you like things to be different in your life? Really visualise how you want your life to be, and the transformation you want to create through this next lunar cycle, and beyond. Maybe you've realised that you'd like a different career or to move to a new town or country? Perhaps your relationship always comes under scrutiny around the dark moon, and you see it's not working as it is? Maybe you always feel exhausted and taken advantage of around a dark moon and it's clear that you need to set better boundaries around your time and energy, saying no to everyone else in order to say yes to yourself every once in a while?

2. Now get clear on why these things matter to you. What difference would it make if you had a new career – would you feel more purposeful or appreciated? Would setting boundaries help you to care for yourself and feel valued as you put you first? Would changes in your relationship make you feel more appreciated or that you could grow together with your partner more as a couple? How would effecting these things these feel? The feeling part is important as it helps you to find and strive for it more in everyday life, so that you know when you are in alignment

with the transformations you are looking to make. As you work with your intentions, you will start to feel more focused, valued, connected – your feelings help you to know you are going in the right direction towards making the intended change.

3. Knowing now what you *do* want, you're ready to set your intentions and declare them in writing. This gives them a huge amount of power (as does saying them out loud). Make sure that your intentions have a lot of heart behind them and that you can really feel the feeling and purpose behind your words. Try to be specific too, so that you can properly connect with the intention – try to make it in one or two clear sentences.

4. These intentions now become your guiding light through the waxing lunar cycle. Allow the feeling of them to infuse your days, helping you to make decisions and show up for yourself differently.

5. Keep checking in with your intentions to make sure that the way you are thinking, speaking, feeling and acting is taking you closer to your intended way of living. Are you embodying your intentions in your daily life?

Some example intentions to get you started:

✴ I intend to put myself first, so that I can take care of my own wellbeing.

✴ I intend to no longer settle for situations that make me unhappy, as I know that I deserve the best.

✴ I intend for communication with my partner to be honest, clear and loving, and that our bond will deepen as a result.

✴ I intend to believe in myself, as I know that I am capable of achieving anything I put my heart and mind to.

✴ I intend to meditate daily as a way to deepen my connection to my inner world and the wisdom and stillness within me.

✴ I intend to find meaning in my work, and for the work I do to be filled with creativity, service and joy.

Dear past,
thank you for all of
the lessons.

Dear future,
I'm ready.

Part 2:

The Journal

CHAPTER 4

New-moon Reflections

HERE IS YOUR space to reflect on each new moon and what this opportunity for a new beginning is bringing you. Taking your dark-moon insights, you'll create new-moon intentions and waxing-moon action points, checking in at the first-quarter moon to ensure you are heading in the right direction.

Aries New Moon

*Focus on new beginnings, finding
purpose and taking action.*

Falls in Aries season, between 21 March and 19 April
Ruled by Mars
Cardinal Fire sign
Symbol: the Ram

You'll find the date of the next Aries new moon on my
website: kirstygallagher.com

Date of Aries new moon ....

Happy astrological new year! Aries season kicks off the astrological year, making the Aries new moon one of the most
powerful for starting over and setting intentions. This moon
falls at the beginning of spring, when everything around us
in nature seems to be shaking off the cobwebs and bursting
back into life, encouraging us to bring some of that same
awakening, blossoming and growth into our personal lives.

Aries lights up a fire in your belly and brings passion, inspiration and motivation to move forward and create much-needed change, whether a new career direction, a big life transition – such as different living circumstances or relationship status – or a promise to begin to believe in yourself more. The Aries moon energy will help you to be much clearer on what you actually want from your life and will bring the courage, will and desire to go after it.

A deeply intuitive sign, Aries will help you to tap into your deepest instincts, visceral desires and your passions and aims in life. Aries vitality will have you stepping up to take charge, becoming the leading role in your own life. It's an enthusiastic sign that brings a fiery dose of get-up-and-go, encouraging you to assert yourself and really chase what your heart desires.

On the flip side, this moon can feel quite intense and bring emotional outbursts, especially if you have been deliberately avoiding the fact that you need new beginnings, ignoring that niggling persistent inner voice. You may find the Aries ram can literally ram you into action, helping you to see a route forward. This moon serves as a wake-up call to what hasn't been working in your life, giving you clarity, focus and direction towards the life you want.

If you don't feel that the year has quite brought you all that you had hoped for, this is a great chance to 'start over'. The traditional new year has never resonated with me personally – I've always found it hard to set intentions and dream in the midst of cold, dark winter! For me, the start of the astrological new year is when I'm inspired by nature coming to life all around me, encouraging me to do the same in my own life. So what do you want to create for yourself in this next astrological new year? Use this fiery moon of action and enthusiasm to look at your life and where you need change and new beginnings – then use this supercharged lunar energy for setting intentions and making things happen.

☾ Dark-moon check-in

Look back at the last full moon: what has shifted for you and what have you let go of since then?

....

....

....

....

....

....

....

What emotions have you been experiencing in the last few days and what have they been showing you?

....

....

....

....

....

....

....

☾ The Aries new-moon soul reflections

The Aries new moon gives you an inner drive to start something new. Taking inspiration from spring all around you, which areas of your life feel as though they need some fresh, new energy or growth brought to them?

....

....

....

....

....

....

....

How would you describe the year so far? Are you really going after what you want – and if not, why not?

....

....

....

....

....

....

....

This moon wants you to live life to the full. Is there one dream you have always put on hold? What steps can you take towards this under this new moon?

....

....

....

....

....

....

....

What emotions have you experienced over this moon? Maybe a fire in your belly to move on with your life – a wake-up call to what isn't working, or anger and frustration around opportunities missed? What are these emotions showing you?

....

....

....

....

....

....

....

Using this supercharged first sign of the zodiac moon energy, what three intentions are you going to set yourself for the next astrological year?

1...

....

2...

....

3...

....

MY INSIGHTS, FEELINGS, GUIDANCE AND WISDOM FROM THE ARIES NEW MOON

....

....

....

....

....

....

....

☾ My Aries new-moon intentions are:

1...

....

2...

....

3...

....

☾ The waxing-moon phase

Three actions I will take during the waxing moon to help take me closer to my new-moon intentions:

1...

....

2...

....

3...

....

☾ First-quarter-moon check-in

What seems to be falling into place or coming together, taking you closer to your new-moon intentions?

....

....

....

....

....

....

....

What seems to be difficult or challenging, and are any doubts and fears surfacing?

....

....

....

....

....

....

....

Taurus New Moon

Focus on slowing down, self-care,
stability and abundance.

Falls in Taurus season, between 20 April and 20 May
Ruled by Venus
Fixed Earth sign
Symbol: the Bull

You'll find the date of the next Taurus new moon on my website: kirstygallagher.com

Date of Taurus new moon ....

The first earth sign of the zodiac, the Taurus new moon comes along to help you to slow down, get present and grounded and find your roots. This intrinsically feminine and earthy new moon offers you a stable, safe sanctuary in which to process and plan.

Taurus wants you to find a stability and security in life that comes not from anything external, but from deep within you

– from standing in your own truth and power and from knowing, trusting and connecting with who you truly are. This moon wants to show you what or who you are attached to and rely on too much, and help you to realise that true stability, safety and security in life come from a deep inner connection and trust in yourself and your abilities and strength.

This Taurus moon will help you to align with your own internal rhythm and a way of life that works for you, rather than always being set by others and their needs and external influences. Being all about self-care, Taurus will show you how to put yourself first. If this is something you struggle with, then this is the moon for you to find the self-worth and self-love that will help you begin to do it.

This is not a new moon for action, but rather slowing right down, getting still and quiet and listening to and drawing on your own inner wisdom and resources. From here, being in this present-moment reality, this Taurus moon will help you to prepare for change, deciding what you want to create for your future and making things a reality. Taurus will further help you to create rituals and routines that steadily take you closer to your dreams.

Taurus will bring you back down to earth, connecting you with your body and anything and everything that will make you feel nourished and grounded. Taurus enjoys the sensual pleasures in life – the home comforts – and will help you to connect to your senses deeply, including your sixth sense. This makes this a wonderful moon for inviting in abundance of all kinds – from money to more pleasure, joy, happiness or self-care.

☾ Dark-Moon check-in

Look back at the last full moon: what has shifted for you and what have you let go of since then?

....

....

....

....

....

....

What emotions have you been experiencing in the last few days and what have they been showing you?

....

....

....

....

....

....

....

☾ The Taurus new-moon soul reflections

How can you find true stability and security within you? How can you begin to believe and trust in yourself more?

....

....

....

....

....

....

....

How can you begin to prioritise self-care and looking after *you*? Do you need more time alone? Better boundaries around taking care of everyone else first? Perhaps a weekly appointment for a massage? Or even just a few hours a week to curl up on the sofa with a good book? What does self-care mean to you?

....

....

....

....

....

....

....

Where are you always rushing in life? How can you slow down and become more present?

....

....

....

....

....

....

....

What daily rituals and routines can you put in place to take you closer to the life you dream of? Perhaps a daily meditation or visualisation practice? Affirmations can help you to believe in yourself. Or how about prioritising your studies, reading or learning something new or simply 30 minutes to yourself at the beginning of each day – time to focus on what you need?

....

....

....

....

....

....

....

What kinds of abundance would you like to welcome into your life, and how can you do this?

....

....

....

....

....

....

....

MY INSIGHTS, FEELINGS, GUIDANCE AND WISDOM FROM THE TAURUS NEW MOON

....

....

....

....

....

....

....

☾ My Taurus new-moon intentions are:

1...

....

2...

....

3...

....

☾ The waxing-moon phase

Three actions I will take during the waxing moon to help take me closer to my new-moon intentions:

1...

....

2...

....

3...

....

☾ First-quarter-moon check-in

What seems to be falling into place or coming together, taking you closer to your new-moon intentions?

....

....

....

....

....

....

....

What seems to be difficult or challenging, and are any doubts and fears surfacing?

....

....

....

....

....

....

....

Gemini New Moon

Focus on change, ideas and inspiration,
taking action and moving forward.

Falls in Gemini season, between 21 May and 20 June
Ruled by Mercury
Mutable Air sign
Symbol: the Twins

You'll find the date of the next Gemini new moon on my website: kirstygallagher.com

Date of Gemini new moon ....

Gemini is a real change-maker moon and comes to help you to move forward. This is the moon for you if you have known for a while that things in your life need to be different, but have been afraid or uncertain of how to make it happen.

If you have been avoiding change, you may find the few days running up to this moon quite unsettling, with a feeling of restlessness and being trapped, with an underlying anxiety. That's how this moon will get your attention, so if you are experiencing heightened emotions, notice the areas of your life that are causing you to feel this way and why. If you are feeling the emotion or exhaustion or intensity of this moon, be sure of this: you are simply being called into all that you are capable of, and you need to step up and claim it.

This moon will bring inspired insights and light-bulb moments – what you want to be different, and how, will become suddenly so obvious to you. And to help you with this, the Gemini new moon will bring an influx of ideas, inspiration and enthusiasm and a desire for knowledge and information and connections.

With the curious nature of Gemini spurring you on, you'll find new ways of looking at your problems and limitations will seem to lift. This moon will enable you to connect the dots, see what you did not see before and realise how you can do things differently. Your instincts and intuition will be strong under this moon, so listen to them. This moon will give you the courage to make change and the tools you need to do it.

This is a light, airy and freedom-seeking new moon. It's a moon of connection, communication and sharing. It wants you to step into your truest authenticity and share your gifts with the world, whispering to you to take that leap of faith.

☾ Dark-moon check-in

Look back at the last full moon: what has shifted for you and what have you let go of since then?

....

....

....

....

....

....

....

What emotions have you been experiencing in the last few days and what have they been showing you?

....

....

....

....

....

....

....

☾ The Gemini new-moon soul reflections

What ideas, inspiration and desires are coming to you right now?

....

....

....

....

....

....

....

What did you not see before that is now clear? How can you look at your problems and possibilities in a different way?

....

....

....

....

....

....

....

What feels out of alignment, or as though it is not currently working for you? Which parts of your life do you feel most unsettled in? These may be areas to consider making changes in under this Gemini new moon.

....

....

....

....

....

....

....

What connections, information, knowledge or help do you need to make any relevant changes happen?

....

....

....

....

....

....

....

Are you ready to take the leap of faith required to move forwards in your life with the Gemini new moon?

....

....

....

....

....

....

....

MY INSIGHTS, FEELINGS, GUIDANCE AND WISDOM FROM THE GEMINI NEW MOON

....

....

....

....

....

....

....

☾ My Gemini new-moon intentions are:

1...

....

2...

....

3...

....

☾ The waxing-moon phase

Three actions I will take during the waxing moon to help take me closer to my new-moon intentions:

1...

....

2...

....

3...

....

☾ First-quarter-moon check-in

What seems to be falling into place or coming together, taking you closer to your new-moon intentions?

....

....

....

....

....

....

....

What seems to be difficult or challenging, and are any doubts and fears surfacing?

....

....

....

....

....

....

....

Cancer New Moon

Focus on working with your emotions,
finding an inner and outer security and
embracing your vulnerability.

♋

Falls in Cancer season, between 21 June and 22 July
Ruled by the Moon
Cardinal Water sign
Symbol: the Crab

You'll find the date of the next Cancer new moon on my website: kirstygallagher.com

Date of Cancer new moon ....

One of the most emotional moons of the year, you'll certainly feel the ebb and flow (or tidal wave) of your emotions under this one. Cancer is ruled by the moon and marks the beginning of summer, bringing us the summer solstice and transition into the second half of the traditional year.

Your emotions around this moon can be transformative if you work with them, rather than allowing them to consume you (a big Cancer trait is going into fear or survival mode and lashing out with your crab-like claws). Not only will sitting with your emotions help you to develop deep self-awareness of your inner world, but the Cancer moon is also asking you to find security in your life – in both your inner and outer worlds.

It's likely that what you're feeling most emotional about under this moon are the places in your life where you feel most insecure, most unsafe or unseen or vulnerable. Take a mini retreat under this moon, even if it's just an evening alone to be with yourself and take an honest look at your life. What in your outer world needs some attention or change in order for you to feel more secure? And how can you invite in more inner security and trust and belief in yourself? As one of the most nurturing signs of the zodiac, Cancer will help you to hold space for yourself to explore your inner fears and vulnerabilities and find a strength that comes from embracing – not denying – your softness.

In a similar vein, this is a beautiful moon by which to see where you prevent yourself from truly living and experiencing life by closing off to protect yourself. Where have you created a tough, crab-like exterior to help you to cope with life? Where have you become defensive and lost touch with the love and kindness within you? How can you allow yourself to be a little more vulnerable, opening your heart to trust in yourself and life a bit more? As a highly intuitive moon, the Cancer moon will help you to connect back into your inner world to find an inner peace and security that come from self-acceptance and love.

☾ Dark-moon check-in

Look back at the last full moon: what has shifted for you and what have you let go of since then?

....

....

....

....

....

....

What emotions have you been experiencing in the last few days and what have they been showing you?

....

....

....

....

....

....

....

☾ The Cancer new-moon soul reflections

As the Cancer new moon takes you deep into your emotions, what are you feeling most emotional about in your life and why? Really feel what you are feeling.

....

....

....

....

....

....

....

What areas in your outer world need some attention or change in order for you to feel more secure? Work? Relationships? Finances? Home life?

....

....

....

....

....

....

....

What do you feel most insecure about in yourself? And how can you begin to develop more trust and belief in yourself?

....

....

....

....

....

....

....

Can you see any ways in which you have closed yourself off from life or become defensive or created a tough exterior: perhaps you avoid forming relationships or meeting new people? Or you take offence easily, taking things too personally? Are you always the first to walk away when things become difficult?

....

....

....

....

....

....

....

How can you allow yourself to be more vulnerable, not only with yourself but also perhaps those closest to you? Can you share your inner world and what you are feeling a bit more?

....

....

....

....

....

....

....

MY INSIGHTS, FEELINGS, GUIDANCE AND WISDOM FROM THE CANCER NEW MOON

....

....

....

....

....

....

....

☾ My Cancer new-moon intentions are:

1. ....

....

2. ....

....

3. ....

....

☾ The waxing-moon phase

Three actions I will take during the waxing moon to help take me closer to my new-moon intentions:

1. ....

....

2. ....

....

3. ....

....

☽ First-quarter-moon check-in

What seems to be falling into place or coming together, taking you closer to your new-moon intentions?

....

....

....

....

....

....

....

What seems to be difficult or challenging, and are any doubts and fears surfacing?

....

....

....

....

....

....

....

Leo New Moon

Focus on living your life, healing old heartache and connecting back to your heart and its desires.

♌

*Falls in Leo season, between 23 July and 22 August
Ruled by the Sun
Fixed Fire sign
Symbol: the Lion*

You'll find the date of the next Leo new moon on my website: kirstygallagher.com

Date of Leo new moon ....

Ruled by the sun, the Leo moon brings an immense amount of energy, light and healing. Leo wants you to shine big, bright and bold. Leo will call you to step into your power and to begin to actually live your life. No more waiting for this or that. No more if, buts, maybes and whens. Your life is a precious gift to be lived, loved, explored and experienced and the Leo new moon will help you to do this.

Leo rules the heart and wants you to be able to embrace and shine your full light, which may mean first of all facing all that remains unhealed, hidden and avoided. That makes this a wonderful moon for healing old heartache and anything that you have been carrying around from the past, so that you can instead open your heart again and begin to look forward to a bright future.

This moon will help you to get in touch with your heart's real desires and what makes you come alive, encouraging you to propel yourself and your talents and gifts out into the spotlight a bit more. Where do you always keep yourself hidden? How can you allow your light to shine a bit more and share all you have to offer with the world? This Leo new moon is here to remind you of your courage, your strength. It's your energetic cheerleader telling you that you've got this: you can do it, you are on purpose and you have the brightest light to shine.

Leo also wants to remind you that life should be fun. Leo brings a childlike vigour that's inspired by just about anything and everything. Allow this energy to remind you of what life was like before all the responsibilities and fears and opinions and 'reality' got in the way. This is a moon to invite more fun and adventure back into your life.

This moon will help you to connect back to the joy, light and happiness in life, so it is one passionate, love-filled, generous and heart-opening new moon. This is a time to truly follow your heart, your passions, your love and go after what lights you up – and Leo is here to tell you that you shine the brightest when you allow yourself to live in this way.

☾ Dark-moon check-in

Look back at the last full moon: what has shifted for you and what have you let go of since then?

....

....

....

....

....

....

....

What emotions have you been experiencing in the last few days and what have they been showing you?

....

....

....

....

....

....

....

☾ The Leo new-moon soul reflections

Where have you been putting your life on hold, waiting for this or that to change?

....

....

....

....

....

....

....

What old heartaches or disappointments have you been carrying around in your heart? How can you connect to your heart a bit more each day?

....

....

....

....

....

....

....

What talents and gifts do you have? Make a list of all the things you are really good at and what you have to offer the world.

....

....

....

....

....

....

....

Where do you always keep yourself hidden: do you never speak up for yourself, share your talents and gifts or celebrate your wins? How can you allow yourself to shine your light a little more?

....

....

....

....

....

....

....

How can you invite more fun, adventure and play into your daily life?

....

....

....

....

....

....

....

MY INSIGHTS, FEELINGS, GUIDANCE AND WISDOM FROM THE LEO NEW MOON

....

....

....

....

....

....

....

☾ My Leo new-moon intentions are:

1...

....

2...

....

3...

....

☾ The waxing-moon phase

Three actions I will take during the waxing moon to help take me closer to my new-moon intentions:

1...

....

2...

....

3...

....

☾ First-quarter-moon check-in

What seems to be falling into place or coming together, taking you closer to your new-moon intentions?

....

....

....

....

....

....

What seems to be difficult or challenging, and are any doubts and fears surfacing?

....

....

....

....

....

....

....

Virgo New Moon

Focus on moving forward, practical next steps and an action plan for healing the inner critic.

Falls in Virgo season, between 23 August and 22 September
Ruled by Mercury
Mutable Earth sign
Symbol: the Virgin

You'll find the date of the next Virgo new moon on my website: kirstygallagher.com

Date of Virgo new moon ....

The Virgo new moon comes along to help you to move forward, not only into autumn, but also in your life. This moon always tends to have a 'back-to-school' feel, as it ushers us out of summer and brings a sense of wanting to get work and other things done. With this moon, it will feel like a way forward is becoming clear.

This new moon brings earthy strength and stability, asking

you to grow roots and set foundations for what you want to become and for the dreams and intentions you want to bring into physical reality in your life for the rest of the year. Virgo will show you practical next steps and bring a logical plan, with all the information, knowledge and support that you need to be able to easily move forward.

You'll find you have an uncanny ability to immediately know what will and won't work under this moon and an intuitive knowing of just what needs to be done to get you to where you want to go. Analytical Virgo energy can be quite transformative in helping you to see the truth, and what you may have missed before.

Anxiety levels, overthinking and the inner critic can be high around this moon so make sure you don't get lost in them. Instead, schedule self-care and healing practices into your day to support you – things like yoga, sharing your worries (with a close friend or someone you trust), meditation or a gratitude list. The sign of the healer, Virgo will allow you to see where anxieties and self-criticism hold you back from going after what you want and help you to work on healing them, so they can't do that any more.

Use this Virgo new moon to get very clear and focused on what you want from the remainder of this year and moving into the start of next. Make your intentions clear, make lists, make an action plan and go for it!

☾ Dark-moon check-in

Look back at the last full moon: what has shifted for you and what have you let go of since then?

....

....

....

....

....

....

....

What emotions have you been experiencing in the last few days and what have they been showing you?

....

....

....

....

....

....

....

☾ The Virgo new-moon soul reflections

What dreams and intentions do you want to bring into physical reality in your life for the rest of the year?

....

....

....

....

....

....

....

What practical support or information do you need to make this happen? Do you have to study or research something or need help from someone in particular?

....

....

....

....

....

....

....

Are you feeling anxious and self-critical around this moon? Can you see how perhaps these same anxieties and that inner critic have held you back before?

....

....

....

....

....

....

....

What daily self-healing practices and rituals can you put in place – yoga, gratitude lists, meditation, affirmations or time in nature, for example?

....

....

....

....

....

....

....

What is your action plan – what practical next steps can you take to help you move forward?

....

....

....

....

....

....

....

MY INSIGHTS, FEELINGS, GUIDANCE AND WISDOM FROM THE VIRGO NEW MOON

....

....

....

....

....

....

....

☾ My Virgo new-moon intentions are:

1..

....

2..

....

3..

....

☾ The waxing-moon phase

Three actions I will take during the waxing moon to help take me closer to my new-moon intentions:

1..

....

2..

....

3..

....

☾ First-quarter-moon check-in

What seems to be falling into place or coming together, taking you closer to your new-moon intentions?

....

....

....

....

....

....

....

What seems to be difficult or challenging, and are any doubts and fears surfacing?

....

....

....

....

....

....

....

Libra New Moon

*Focus on self-care, autumn new beginnings
and finding balance in your life.*

Falls in Libra season, between 23 September and 22 October
Ruled by Venus
Cardinal Air sign
Symbol: the Scales

You'll find the date of the next Libra new moon on my website: kirstygallagher.com

Date of Libra new moon ....

The first new moon after the autumn equinox, this is here to help you to set your intentions for the autumn season. While every new moon brings the chance of a new beginning, change is definitely in the autumn air with this one. All around you, Mother Nature is shedding and transforming and inspiring you to do the same.

You may feel a real need to start to take care of yourself

under this moon, not just on the outside but on the inside too. The more you can slow down, take care of yourself and make your inner world a priority, the more you will be able to align with the inner whispers of what your heart wants and allow that to guide you through the new season.

Relationships always come under the moonlight with a Libra moon and so, just like the leaves from the trees, you may find challenging or outgrown relationships falling away. Allow that. Just be mindful that Libra doesn't like conflict, and so it may be tempting to make excuses for people and their behaviours. All you are doing here though is smoothing over cracks and holding on to the dead leaves (relationships), leaving no space for beautiful new ones to flourish. Be honest with yourself, and others, and use the inspiration of nature all around you to let go.

The Libra new moon is all about restoring balance in all areas of your life, especially after the busyness of summer. This is a wonderful moon to take a life review and see where you have allowed yourself to get out of alignment. What areas of your life are taking up too much of your time, energy and effort? Where are you giving too much of yourself away to your own detriment? And how can you begin to restore the equilibrium in your life?

☾ Dark-moon check-in

Look back at the last full moon: what has shifted for you and what have you let go of since then?

....

....

....

....

....

....

....

What emotions you have been experiencing in the last few days and what have they been showing you?

....

....

....

....

....

....

....

☾ The Libra new-moon soul reflections

How can you slow down and commit to some real self-care under this new moon?

....

....

....

....

....

....

....

What in your life do you need to let go of and release as we move into autumn?

....

....

....

....

....

....

....

Are there any relationships in your life that are challenging or outgrown? Do you seem to always be making excuses for other people's behaviour?

....

....

....

....

....

....

....

What areas of your life feel most off-kilter right now? How can you address this?

....

....

....

....

....

....

....

What life changes do you want to make in this autumn season?

....

....

....

....

....

....

....

MY INSIGHTS, FEELINGS, GUIDANCE AND WISDOM FROM THE LIBRA NEW MOON

....

....

....

....

....

....

....

☾ My Libra new-moon intentions are:

1..

....

2..

....

3..

....

☾ The waxing-moon phase

Three actions I will take during the waxing moon to help take me closer to my new-moon intentions:

1..

....

2..

....

3..

....

◖ First-quarter-moon check-in

What seems to be falling into place or coming together, taking you closer to your new-moon intentions?

....

....

....

....

....

....

....

What seems to be difficult or challenging, and are any doubts and fears surfacing?

....

....

....

....

....

....

....

Scorpio New Moon

*Focus on personal growth, overcoming
fears and making big changes.*

♏

*Falls in Scorpio season, between 23 October and 21 November
Ruled by Mars and Pluto
Fixed Water sign
Symbol: the Scorpion*

You'll find the date of the next Scorpio new moon on my website: kirstygallagher.com

Date of Scorpio new moon ....

Scorpio is the magician, the alchemist of the zodiac, and this moon comes along to help you transform your shadows into your greatest strengths, your fears into friends and your self-doubt into self-belief. This moon will bring the courage and strength to transform your life, and a fearlessness to go after what you really want.

Emotionally intense, this moon will take you into all the

areas in your life that you avoid and are usually afraid to confront or alter. You'll be asked to look within you at the voices of doubt and doom that keep you stuck, and the parts of yourself that you try to run and hide from, so that you can face them, embrace them and bring them to the light for healing. This is a new moon for personal growth and transformation and becoming the alchemist and change-maker in your own life.

When you get beneath the noise of the mind and human doubts and fears, the Scorpio new moon will help you connect with and trust your inner wisdom, instincts and intuition and to know what you truly desire from life. You'll be encouraged to push boundaries, go beyond what you thought was possible and take the road less travelled. This moon brings a relentless determination and focus to following your heart's desires and an ability to easily overcome obstacles or difficulties that seem to stand in the way.

All that makes this a wonderful moon under which to begin something new or make a change that has previously scared or seemed too big for you. Scorpio brings an alchemical magic that will help to awaken you to your own inner power and say yes to all of the possibilities that life has to offer on the other side of fear.

☾ Dark-moon check-in

Look back at the last full moon: what has shifted for you and what have you let go of since then?

....

....

....

....

....

....

....

What emotions have you been experiencing in the last few days and what have they been showing you?

....

....

....

....

....

....

....

☾ The Scorpio new-moon soul reflections

What areas of your life have you known that you need to do differently, but been avoiding or too afraid to confront?

....

....

....

....

....

....

....

What voices of doubt and doom always seem to keep you stuck and prevent you from making change?

....

....

....

....

....

....

....

What are your true heart's desires? For every apparent obstacle or difficulty in the way of following your heart's desires, can you write one possibility for how it could be overcome?

....

....

....

....

....

....

....

Can you identify one big change or new thing that you can begin under this moon (or even just some small steps towards it)?

....

....

....

....

....

....

....

What would you say yes to in your life if you had no fears at all?

....

....

....

....

....

....

....

MY INSIGHTS, FEELINGS, GUIDANCE AND
WISDOM FROM THE SCORPIO NEW MOON

....

....

....

....

....

....

....

☾ My Scorpio new-moon intentions are:

1..

....

2..

....

3..

....

☾ The waxing-moon phase

Three actions I will take during the waxing moon to help take me closer to my new-moon intentions:

1..

....

2..

....

3..

....

☾ First-quarter-moon check-in

What seems to be falling into place or coming together, taking you closer to your new-moon intentions?

....

....

....

....

....

....

....

What seems to be difficult or challenging, and are any doubts and fears surfacing?

....

....

....

....

....

....

....

Sagittarius New Moon

*Focus on reviewing and reflecting on the
year, finding faith and taking chances.*

*Falls in Sagittarius season, between 22 November
and 21 December
Ruled by Jupiter
Mutable Fire sign
Symbol: the Archer*

You'll find the date of the next Sagittarius new moon on my
website: kirstygallagher.com

Date of Sagittarius new moon ....

Bringing enthusiasm, adventure and wanderlust, this new
moon is a huge opportunity for taking chances at a new
beginning. This is the final full lunar cycle of the traditional year and gives you an opening to review and reflect
on the year gone by. Sagittarius seeks to find meaning in
life and will help you to see the lessons that have brought

you to this point – what you have learned and how you have grown.

This moon will help you to find an unwavering faith in where your journey is taking you and what you want to create going forward in your life. Anything can be achieved under a Sagittarius moon, so there could not be a better time for putting in place the changes and new beginnings that you want for not only the ending of this year but also into the next one.

Sagittarius has an insatiable appetite for wandering, exploring, learning, expanding and will help you to seek and find all that you need to support you in your growth and evolution. This is a moon that brings the inspiration and inner wisdom that you need to be able to see a way forward. It will expand your vision and open you up not only to your full potential, but also to how you can use it in the world. You'll suddenly be able to see possibilities that you perhaps couldn't before.

As a sign of freedom and independence, this moon will show you where you have held back and what you have put on hold all year: those dreams you never got around to because of the myriad excuses. Use the expansive, inspiring energy of this moon to find your adventurous spirit, to be bold, to believe in and take a chance on yourself and life – and to wholeheartedly go after what you want.

☾ Dark-moon check-in

Look back at the last full moon: what has shifted for you and what have you let go of since then?

....

....

....

....

....

....

....

What emotions have you been experiencing in the last few days and what have they been showing you?

....

....

....

....

....

....

....

☾ The Sagittarius new-moon soul reflections

What are the greatest lessons that this year has taught you and how have you grown through these experiences?

....

....

....

....

....

....

....

How do you want the end of this traditional year and the start of the next to be different for you? What would you do if you trusted that anything could be achieved?

....

....

....

....

....

....

....

What do you need to support you in these changes? Do you need to learn a new skill, ask for assistance, take some time out on an adventure to expand your horizons?

....

....

....

....

....

....

....

What dreams did you put on hold this year or never get around to starting and why?

....

....

....

....

....

....

....

THE LUNAR LIVING JOURNAL

Can you identify one thing you can do under this moon to take a chance and really start to go after what you want?

....

....

....

....

....

....

....

MY INSIGHTS, FEELINGS, GUIDANCE AND WISDOM FROM THE SAGITTARIUS NEW MOON

....

....

....

....

....

....

....

☽ My Sagittarius new-moon intentions are:

1..

....

2..

....

3..

....

☽ The waxing-moon phase

Three actions I will take during the waxing moon to help take me closer to my new-moon intentions:

1..

....

2..

....

3..

....

THE LUNAR LIVING JOURNAL

☾ First-quarter-moon check-in

What seems to be falling into place or coming together, taking
you closer to your new-moon intentions?

....

....

....

....

....

....

....

What seems to be difficult or challenging, and are any doubts
and fears surfacing?

....

....

....

....

....

....

....

Capricorn New Moon

Focus on laying stable foundations, getting clear on what you want and creating an action plan.

Falls in Capricorn season, between 22 December and 19 January
Ruled by Saturn
Cardinal Earth sign
Symbol: the Goat

You'll find the date of the next Capricorn new moon on my website: kirstygallagher.com

Date of Capricorn new moon ....

Grounded and earthy, this new moon brings the opportunity to lay the foundations on which you will build the next traditional year. This is a moon to get very clear on what you truly want to ensure that you don't keep running on autopilot and repeating similar stories, patterns and situations into the new year and beyond.

This new moon shows you that it's not enough to simply dream and set intentions for the year ahead; you need to take action too: if you want things to be different in this next year, you need to do things differently. These changes must start with you, from within. You have to set a clear focus on what you want and what you will – and won't – accept. Your inner structures of self-worth, self-belief, self-love and self-respect need to be strong in order for you to begin the journey of following your dreams. Once these are in place, Capricorn will bring you a determination to reach your life goals like never before.

Capricorn wants you to take your focus off what hasn't been working, and instead put all your energy into what you want and how you will get there. Consider your career, financial, relationship and personal goals for the year ahead.

Use the energies of this moon to contemplate what you want to experience, share, create and bring to life this next year; use them to make an action plan – both short-term and longer-term. Break your plan down into small, manageable steps – what action do you need to take to move you towards your goals? Allow ambitious, motivating Capricorn to show you the way.

☾ Dark-moon check-in

Look back at the last full moon: what has shifted for you and what have you let go of since then?

....

....

....

....

....

....

What emotions have you been experiencing in the last few days and what have they been showing you?

....

....

....

....

....

....

....

☾ The Capricorn new-moon soul reflections

How would you like your life to be by the end of this calendar year? Looking ahead, what would be different – and how?

....
....
....
....
....
....
....

What do you not want to repeat from last year and how can you do things differently to help achieve this?

....
....
....
....
....
....
....

Make a short- and long-term action plan for the year ahead. What daily, weekly and monthly steps do you need to be taking?

....

....

....

....

....

....

....

What are your career, financial, relationship and personal goals for the year ahead?

....

....

....

....

....

....

....

Which areas of yourself need some work to ensure you can follow your dreams? Do you need to be doing daily work around self-belief or self-worth?

....

....

....

....

....

....

....

MY INSIGHTS, FEELINGS, GUIDANCE AND WISDOM FROM THE CAPRICORN NEW MOON

....

....

....

....

....

....

....

☾ My Capricorn new-moon intentions are:

1...

....

2...

....

3...

....

☾ The waxing-moon phase

Three actions I will take during the waxing moon to help take me closer to my new-moon intentions:

1...

....

2...

....

3...

....

☾ First-quarter-moon check-in

What seems to be falling into place or coming together, taking you closer to your new-moon intentions?

....

....

....

....

....

....

....

What seems to be difficult or challenging, and are any doubts and fears surfacing?

....

....

....

....

....

....

....

Aquarius New Moon

*Focus on the bigger picture of your life, your gifts
and realising your wildest hopes and dreams.*

*Falls in Aquarius season, between 20 January and 18 February
Ruled by Uranus and Saturn
Fixed Air sign
Symbol: the Water Bearer*

You'll find the date of the next Aquarius new moon on my
website: kirstygallagher.com

Date of Aquarius new moon ....

This airy, freedom-seeking moon falls around Imbolc (1st and
2nd February), the cross-quarter festival that celebrates the first
emergence out of winter towards spring. Just as Imbolc starts
to stir all of the seeds of life that have been buried deep within
the soil over winter, this moon will stir things within you too.
It brings with it a visionary quality to help you look towards
the future and envision the bigger picture of your life.

Aquarius is the rebel of the zodiac, the sign that takes you into humanitarian-focused action and shows you that you have been given gifts, passions and talents for a reason, and that the world needs you. You may have been telling yourself for the longest time that you don't have anything to offer, that you can't make a difference in the world and that you can't follow your dream because of x, y and z – but Aquarius is here to tell you that you can. And you must.

One thing that Aquarius holds dearer than anything is freedom. And so anything that stifles your freedom or your ability to live your bigger-picture dreams will be obvious under this moon. This is a moon to allow your wildest hopes and dreams to be realised, and your belief in them to be bigger than all of the small worries and doubts that so often get in the way. This moon will help you to shake things up in your life to create awakening and positive change, so that you can follow the direction of your dreams. It's a moon to trust in yourself and the flow of life.

☾ Dark-moon check-in

Look back at the last full moon: what has shifted for you and what have you let go of since then?

....

....

....

....

....

....

....

What emotions have you been experiencing in the last few days and what have they been showing you?

....

....

....

....

....

....

....

☾ The Aquarius new-moon soul reflections

What are your greatest gifts, passions and talents in life? Do you put these to good use in your daily life?

....

....

....

....

....

....

....

What are your wildest hopes and dreams for yourself? Dream big with this reflection.

....

....

....

....

....

....

....

What 'small stuff' and excuses do you always allow to get in the way of being able to follow your dreams?

....

....

....

....

....

....

....

What do you feel is stifling your freedom and ability to live the life you want?

....

....

....

....

....

....

....

What areas of your life need shaking up or some positive change?

....

....

....

....

....

....

....

MY INSIGHTS, FEELINGS, GUIDANCE AND WISDOM FROM THE AQUARIUS NEW MOON

....

....

....

....

....

....

....

☾ My Aquarius new-moon intentions are:

1...

....

2...

....

3...

....

☾ The waxing-moon phase

Three actions I will take during the waxing moon to help take me closer to my new-moon intentions:

1...

....

2...

....

3...

....

☾ First-quarter-moon check-in

What seems to be falling into place or coming together, taking you closer to your new-moon intentions?

....

....

....

....

....

....

....

What seems to be difficult or challenging, and are any doubts and fears surfacing?

....

....

....

....

....

....

....

Pisces New Moon

*Focus on endings, forgiveness and
connecting to your intuition.*

*Falls in Pisces season, between 19 February and 20 March
Ruled by Neptune and Jupiter
Mutable Water sign
Symbol: the Fish*

You'll find the date of the next Pisces new moon on my website: kirstygallagher.com

Date of Pisces new moon ....

Pisces is the last sign of the zodiac, and so this new moon is like the final dive into the depths, so you can enter spring cleansed and ready for new beginnings. It's here to help you reflect on the astrological year gone by, to find closure, completion and direction in your life.

This may be the moon under which you finally stop allowing people to treat or speak to you in certain ways. It may be the moon under which you release the ties that bind you to the past and no longer permit yourself to be pulled back in, so that you can see what else is waiting out there for you; or when you finally stop letting the opinions, views and behaviour of others affect you.

This is a moon of forgiveness, which will bring the deepest healing imaginable. You cannot move on from the past if you are still being pulled back into it by resentment, continuing to be triggered by it, ruminating or wanting to change it. Forgiveness does not mean that you are saying what happened was right. It is simply that you are no longer willing to keep yourself stuck in the past, carrying it around with you.

The endings to create new beginnings that this moon is asking of you are also focused on the inner you. This moon is about ending your self-sabotaging cycles, your limiting relationship with your fears and the amount of attention you give to the doubting voices in your mind – the voices that are saying you 'can't'.

Your connection to your intuition – your 'higher self' – will be strong under this moon, as will your ability to fully dream your dreams. This moon will help you to feel and see the dreams that live deep within your heart and soul. If your life could be any way that you wanted it to be, what would that look like, feel like, sound like? The more power you can give to your dreams, the more likely it is that they will come true.

☾ Dark-moon check-in

Look back at the last full moon: what has shifted for you and what have you let go of since then?

....

....

....

....

....

....

....

What emotions have you been experiencing in the last few days and what have they been showing you?

....

....

....

....

....

....

....

☾ The Pisces new-moon soul reflections

What keeps you tied to the past? What still triggers you? What do you ruminate over and wish you could change?

....

....

....

....

....

....

....

What endings do you need to create for yourself under this moon? What in your life is no longer working for you?

....

....

....

....

....

....

....

Who and what do you need to forgive in order to heal and move on?

....

....

....

....

....

....

....

In what life areas do you seem to self-sabotage or experience the most doubt or fear?

....

....

....

....

....

....

....

Can you identify one life dream that you currently have?
Describe it here in as much detail as you can.

....

....

....

....

....

....

....

MY INSIGHTS, FEELINGS, GUIDANCE AND
WISDOM FROM THE PISCES NEW MOON

....

....

....

....

....

....

....

☾ My Pisces new-moon intentions are:

1...

....

2...

....

3...

....

☾ The waxing-moon phase

Three actions I will take during the waxing moon to help take me closer to my new-moon intentions:

1...

....

2...

....

3...

....

☾ First-quarter-moon check-in

What seems to be falling into place or coming together, taking you closer to your new-moon intentions?

....

....

....

....

....

....

....

What seems to be difficult or challenging, and are any doubts and fears surfacing?

....

....

....

....

....

....

....

CHAPTER 5

Full-moon Reflections

HERE IS YOUR space to reflect on each full moon and what this opportunity for completion and closure is bringing you. You'll celebrate your wins, declare what you are releasing, set waning-moon action points and check in at the last-quarter moon to ensure you are heading in the right direction.

Aries Full Moon

Focus on letting go of limitations, taking back your power and reigniting your passion and desires.

Falls in Libra season, between 23 September and 22 October
Ruled by Mars
Cardinal Fire sign
Symbol: the Ram

You'll find the date of the next Aries full moon on my website: kirstygallagher.com

Date of Aries full moon ....

Big, bold, fiery and full of strength, the Aries full moon brings huge energy and, very often, heightened emotions. The emotions that arise under this full moon are a great indicator of the life areas you need to work on and what holds you back. The first full moon following the autumn equinox, this full moon is here to propel you forward into a change of direction, of season, of life.

The first sign of the zodiac is once again here to ignite your inner fire and create new beginnings towards living the life that you want. This moon will help you to see clearly where you have allowed your needs, desires, passion and dreams to go unmet, ignoring those inner niggles and the call of your heart.

This moon is a call to action – a cry for attention to all of the ways you have allowed yourself to be held back and your fears to be bigger than your faith. This full moon is here to help you let go of everything that is in your way.

The Aries moon will allow you to remember your power and your right to the life you want and deserve. It will urge you to push through the excuses and reservations, giving you the courage to confront what hasn't been working in your life for so long. It will help you to challenge yourself, take risks and take action towards something that has been scaring you.

This full moon calls you into your greatness and real purpose on this earth, releasing all that limits and prevents you from shining bright and living a full life.

☾ The Aries full-moon soul reflections

Which life areas are your emotions guiding you to pay attention to? Are they calling you to take a look at your romantic relationships, your career, your friendships, your health or your social life?

....

....

....

....

....

....

....

Where have you allowed your own needs and dreams to go unmet?

....

....

....

....

....

....

....

How can you begin to have more faith in yourself, your dreams and life? Can you remind yourself of past successes, your strengths and abilities – the times when things have worked out well? Tell yourself daily how much you believe in yourself.

....

....

....

....

....

....

....

Can you identify one thing you need to release from your life that always limits and holds you back?

....

....

....

....

....

....

....

This full moon is here to remind you that you deserve to live the life that you desire. How can you take back your power and take action towards something that you really want?

....

....

....

....

....

....

....

MY INSIGHTS, FEELINGS, GUIDANCE AND
WISDOM FROM THE ARIES FULL MOON

....

....

....

....

....

....

....

☾ On this Aries full moon, I am celebrating:

....

....

....

....

....

....

....

☾ Under the Aries full moon, I am releasing:

1..

....

2..

....

3..

....

☾ The waning-moon phase

Three actions I will take under the waning moon to help me release these things:

1..
....

2..
....

3..
....

☾ Last-quarter-moon check-in

What have you learned and experienced so far through the lunar cycle?

....
....
....
....
....
....
....

What are you ready to heal and release?

....

....

....

....

....

....

....

Taurus Full Moon

*Focus on self-care, an inner review and
anchoring into self-acceptance and worth.*

Falls in Scorpio season, between 23 October and 21 November
Ruled by Venus
Fixed Earth sign
Symbol: the Bull

You'll find the date of the next Taurus full moon on my
website: kirstygallagher.com

Date of Taurus full moon ....

This is a nurturing, nourishing full moon that calls you back
to the earth to find roots and grounding in your life.

This full moon will show you where you have been allowing yourself to get pulled out of alignment, taken on too
much, are feeling overwhelmed or emotionally frazzled and
where, quite simply, enough is enough. There will be a
tendency under this moon to want to stubbornly shut down

completely – resist that, and instead turn your focus back to yourself and self-care, self-care, self-care.

And as you turn your focus back to you, this moon is a beautiful time for a review of your inner world too. The Taurus moon can bring up issues around self-worth. It will shine a light on your deepest insecurities – all of the things you struggle to accept and understand about yourself and what you consider your flaws and weaknesses to be. Like a loving friend, the Taurus moon will provide a safe space for you to allow these things to surface, so you can get to know, accept and love yourself even more. It's through this coming back to yourself that you will find a more secure anchor within you from which to explore what you want and need in your life.

The Taurus moon also brings a focus on to what you stubbornly refuse to change or let go of, and how you can often blame other people or situations for things in your life. Notice anywhere in your life where there is still blame or judgement or where you are being bull-headed. Take back the responsibility, forgiving where necessary (and that sometimes means forgiving yourself).

☾ The Taurus full-moon soul reflections

Where are you currently feeling overwhelmed in your life or emotionally exhausted? Where do you feel enough is enough?

....

....

....

....

....

....

....

How can you truly take care of yourself under this moon? There are so many different versions of self-care – from bubble baths and massage to meditation, time alone, therapy or just completely switching off for a day. What does self-care mean to you? And how can you implement more of that around this full moon?

....

....

....

....

....

....

....

What is surfacing for you around self-worth? What insecurities or so-called weaknesses are making themselves known?

....

....

....

....

....

....

....

How can you invite more self-acceptance and self-love into your life and find a secure anchor in being you? Things like forgiving yourself, accepting the past and being incredibly kind to yourself – especially when your inner critic comes out to play – will all help with this.

....

....

....

....

....

....

....

Where are you stubbornly refusing to change or blaming or judging? Is there anyone or anything that you need to forgive under this moon?

....

....

....

....

....

....

....

MY INSIGHTS, FEELINGS, GUIDANCE AND WISDOM FROM THE TAURUS FULL MOON

....

....

....

....

....

....

....

☾ On this Taurus full moon, I am celebrating:

....

....

....

....

....

....

....

☾ Under the Taurus full moon, I am releasing:

1..

....

2..

....

3..

....

☾ The waning-moon phase

Three actions I will take under the waning moon to help me release these things:

1..
....

2..
....

3..
....

☾ Last-quarter-moon check-in

What have you learned and experienced so far through the lunar cycle?

....
....
....
....
....
....
....

What are you ready to heal and release?

....

....

....

....

....

....

....

Gemini Full Moon

Focus on seeing all that's possible for you, slowing down and gathering knowledge and information.

*Falls in Sagittarius season, between 22
November and 21 December
Ruled by Mercury
Mutable Air sign
Symbol: the Twins*

You'll find the date of the next Gemini full moon on my website: kirstygallagher.com

Date of Gemini full moon ....

Feelings of anxiety, heightened emotion and having so much to do, but you're not sure what or how, often accompany this full moon. The symbol of the twins represents two different personalities in one, and this is never truer than under this moon.

You will find that you get inspiration for a whole new career option, or a glimpse of the happier future you could have if you left a certain situation or relationship; but then doubt, fear and the voice of doom rush in alongside this.

Take a deep breath! This is all happening to help you to find a deeper meaning in your life and show you what is possible, and what also holds you back from those possibilities. Get curious. Gently ask questions: what would life look like if I did make that change? What scares me the most about making it and why? One thing that Gemini loves is change, and this moon will help you to see where you have been avoiding seeing the truth and therefore not making much-needed transformations in your life.

It's important under this moon to slow down and take time to process all the information coming to you, and to do this from an open heart. The more you can remain with your heart and feelings, rather than getting completely lost in the noise in your head, the more insights and wisdom you will receive from this moon.

Gemini loves knowledge and gathering information and you may find that you are being called to learn new skills, to study something new or find a new direction in your life for the next year, perhaps seeing little glimpses of all that's possible and yet to come. Use this moon to let go of all that holds you back and start to put in the groundwork for all that's waiting for you to explore.

☾ The Gemini full-moon soul reflections

What thoughts are you finding your head filled with – perhaps about career, relationships, living arrangements?

....
....
....
....
....
....
....

What much-needed changes are you being shown you need to make in your life right now?

....
....
....
....
....
....
....

What scares you the most about making them and why?

....

....

....

....

....

....

....

How can you slow down under this full moon and stay more connected to your heart?

....

....

....

....

....

....

....

Are you being called to gather more knowledge, skills or information to help you towards these changes?

....

....

....

....

....

....

MY INSIGHTS, FEELINGS, GUIDANCE AND WISDOM FROM THE GEMINI FULL MOON

....

....

....

....

....

....

....

☾ **On this Gemini full moon, I am celebrating:**

....

....

....

....

....

....

....

☾ **Under the Gemini full moon, I am releasing:**

1..

....

2..

....

3..

....

◖ The waning-moon phase

Three actions I will take under the waning moon to help me release these things:

1..

....

2..

....

3..

....

◖ Last-quarter-moon check-in

What have you learned and experienced so far through the lunar cycle?

....

....

....

....

....

....

....

What are you ready to heal and release?

....

....

....

....

....

....

....

Cancer Full Moon

Focus on coming home to yourself, being
emotionally available and listening to your intuition.

Falls in Capricorn season, between 22 December and 19 January
Ruled by the Moon
Cardinal Water sign
Symbol: the Crab

You'll find the date of the next Cancer full moon on my website: kirstygallagher.com

Date of Cancer full moon ....

The moon is fully at home in her sign of Cancer and is calling for *you* to come home completely to yourself. Your way forward into the traditional new year is being lit up by the heartfelt guidance of this nurturing, intuitive, loyal and supportive sign.

This is a full moon that will bring you home to your dreams, visions, purpose, power and all that you are capable of. To get into that purpose and power though, you first have to move past the gatekeepers – aka the emotions, doubts and fears that have you hiding in your Cancer crab-like shell. This full moon is here to help you do just that.

Cancer is representative of true feminine energy and strength, teaching you that shutting down your emotions and creating a shell around yourself for fear of being hurt, judged or rejected is no longer an option if you want to truly transform and find peace and happiness. Embracing and accepting your emotions, being emotionally available, fully present with others and diving into your vulnerability is where your powers really lie.

With the moon in the watery sign of emotions, you're likely to feel that all of your own emotions are pulled to the surface. Rather than get caught up in this turmoil though, this is an opportunity for inner reflection and self-awareness. Sit with these thoughts and emotions, doubts and fears, tune in deeply and see if you can really get to the bottom of where they come from, what they are showing you and how they may have served you in the past? Go deeper: what are you now willing to let go of to become your true, authentic self? What is no longer true for you or serving you? What is in the way of you stepping into your most authentic self and feeling completely at home in who you are?

Your intuition, insight and inner guidance will be at their absolute peak under this moon, so listen to them, trust them, believe them – they will never be wrong.

☾ The Cancer full-moon soul reflections

If you really feel and listen to your emotions, what are they telling/showing you? Can you get to the bottom of where they have come from or what they have been trying to protect you from?

....

....

....

....

....

....

....

In what areas of your life do you feel most inauthentic and not able to show up as the real you? Are there certain people or situations that seem to make you hide in your shell?

....

....

....

....

....

....

....

What are you finally willing to let go of, so that you can become your true, authentic self? Can you work on worrying less about what others think or on no longer seeking approval or validation from anyone other than you?

....

....

....

....

....

....

....

How can you allow yourself to become more emotionally available and vulnerable with those closest to you? How can you share more of what you feel and need?

....

....

....

....

....

....

....

What are your inner guidance and intuition telling you right now? Are you feeling the call to finally have difficult conversations with someone, walk away from a situation that hasn't been making you feel good or take the first steps towards following a dream?

....

....

....

....

....

....

....

MY INSIGHTS, FEELINGS, GUIDANCE AND WISDOM FROM THE CANCER FULL MOON

....

....

....

....

....

....

....

☾ On this Cancer full moon, I am celebrating:

....

....

....

....

....

....

....

☾ Under the Cancer full moon, I am releasing:

1..

....

2..

....

3..

....

☾ The waning-moon phase

Three actions I will take under the waning moon to help me release these things:

1..
....

2..
....

3..
....

☾ Last-quarter-moon check-in

What have you learned and experienced so far through the lunar cycle?

....
....
....
....
....
....
....

What are you ready to heal and release?

....

....

....

....

....

....

....

Leo Full Moon

Focus on taking centre stage in your life, healing your heart and releasing anything that dims your light.

♌

Falls in Aquarius season, between 20 January and 18 February
Ruled by the Sun
Fixed Fire sign
Symbol: the Lion

You'll find the date of the next Leo full moon on my website: kirstygallagher.com

Date of Leo full moon ....

Fiery, bright and bold, the Leo full moon comes to light up your life and help you to share your individual, unique and most authentic self with the world. Leo wants you to take centre stage in your own life.

Far from making you feel like the king (or queen) of the jungle though, this full moon may feel unsettling and confusing and intensely emotional. You may find yourself ruminating over past hurts and exes, reliving hurtful situations and experiencing misgivings and fears. But all of this has true healing ability and is what's needed to take you to the next level in your life.

This moon will take you straight into your heart for healing, and it's as though anything and everything that can and will pull you off track and leave you feeling a bit vulnerable, raw and doubting is all coming at once. This is to demonstrate the healing that still needs to take place in your heart in order to open it fully – the fears that keep you from completely shining your light, the voice of doubt that prevents you from stepping into the limelight in your life and sharing from your heart all that's yearning to come out.

You cannot step fully into your purpose and power if your inner light is dim. Leo wants you to awaken that flame within you – to clear the obstacles, so that you can truly begin to tune in to what sets your soul on fire and your heart alight.

◖ The Leo full-moon soul reflections

Have you found yourself ruminating over past hurts or memories or feeling a lot of doubt or fear under this moon? Open your heart here and get it all out.

....

....

....

....

....

....

....

What do you feel still needs healing or forgiving or releasing from your heart? What are you still carrying around with you?

....

....

....

....

....

....

....

What prevents you from letting the world know you are here and sharing all of your unique brilliance? Is it self-doubt, fear, worries about what 'they' may say?

....

....

....

....

....

....

....

What puts out your inner fire and makes you shrink back, feeling small and less of yourself?

....

....

....

....

....

....

....

What lights you up and makes you come alive?

....

....

....

....

....

....

MY INSIGHTS, FEELINGS, GUIDANCE AND
WISDOM FROM THE LEO FULL MOON

....

....

....

....

....

....

....

☾ On this Leo full moon, I am celebrating:

....

....

....

....

....

....

....

☾ Under the Leo full moon, I am releasing:

1..

....

2..

....

3..

....

☾ The waning-moon phase

Three actions I will take under the waning moon to help me release these things:

1..

....

2..

....

3..

....

☾ Last-quarter-moon check-in

What have you learned and experienced so far through the lunar cycle?

....

....

....

....

....

....

....

What are you ready to heal and release?

....

....

....

....

....

....

....

Virgo Full Moon

Focus on a healing life review, getting your life in order and making meaningful improvements.

Falls in Pisces season, between 19 February and 20 March
Ruled by Mercury
Mutable Earth sign
Symbol: the Virgin

You'll find the date of the next Virgo full moon on my website: kirstygallagher.com

Date of Virgo full moon ....

Virgo is the sign of the healer, and so this full moon brings a physical, mental, emotional and spiritual life review to help you release all that keeps your wellbeing out of alignment. Very much connected with the earth, this moon wants you to return to a place of feeling grounded, rooted, stable and secure in your life.

Similarly, practical and organised Virgo will help you to sort through any other areas of your life that have been making you feel anxious or frustrated and bring about an urge to declutter your life. What is fraying your nerves around this moon? What feels out of order? What are you constantly overanalysing? Where in your life do you feel most stuck and frustrated? These are the things that need your attention under this moon, and Virgo energy can be quite transformative in helping you to see the truth, and what you may have missed before.

Anxiety and overthinking can be high around this moon, as can a sense of wanting to turn inward and spend time alone, as Virgo helps you begin to put your life in order. Be mindful too of the inner critic and any judgemental thoughts that could make this feel more like an interrogation into all that is 'wrong' in your life. Go gently on yourself and use these energies to help you make lasting, meaningful improvements.

Virgo loves lists and structures and rituals and routines. And so, especially if you are undertaking a life overhaul around this moon, make sure that you put daily self-care and healing practices into your schedule to support you through these changes – like time in nature, getting enough downtime and sleep, daily yoga or gentle exercise, meditation or a gratitude list.

☾ The Virgo full-moon soul reflections

Take a physical, mental, emotional and spiritual life review and notice where you are out of alignment in these areas. What can you do to bring more healing into these parts of your life?

....

....

....

....

....

....

....

What areas of your life need a declutter? This will be made more obvious by what you're feeling the most anxious and frustrated about.

....

....

....

....

....

....

....

What in your life helps you to be most grounded and stable? Is it being in nature? Time with certain people? Having things organised in a certain way? Do more of what makes you feel safe over this moon.

....

....

....

....

....

....

....

What lasting, meaningful improvements do you want to make in your life moving forward?

....

....

....

....

....

....

....

What daily self-care rituals can you commit to over the next few weeks to support you through any changes you are making?

....

....

....

....

....

....

....

MY INSIGHTS, FEELINGS, GUIDANCE AND WISDOM FROM THE VIRGO FULL MOON

....

....

....

....

....

....

....

☾ **On this Virgo full moon, I am celebrating:**

....

....

....

....

....

....

....

☾ **Under the Virgo full moon, I am releasing:**

1..

....

2..

....

3..

....

☾ The waning-moon phase

Three actions I will take under the waning moon to help me release these things:

1..

....

2..

....

3..

....

☾ Last-quarter-moon check-in

What have you learned and experienced so far through the lunar cycle?

....

....

....

....

....

....

....

What are you ready to heal and release?

....

....

....

....

....

....

....

Libra Full Moon

Focus on releasing all that keeps you out of balance, and on self-love, self-care and relationships.

Falls in Aries season, between 21 March and 19 April
Ruled by Venus
Cardinal Air sign
Symbol: the Scales

You'll find the date of the next Libra full moon on my website: kirstygallagher.com

Date of Libra full moon ....

This is the first full moon after the spring equinox, which marks the start of the astrological new year and change in season.

Just as spring is the perfect time for a cleanse, this full moon will help you to reset the scales, as well as find equilibrium between doing and being, pushing and pulling and releasing – so that you are able to do what you *can* do and surrender with trust what you have no control over.

This moon helps to strengthen the relationship you have with yourself and to come back into alignment with your truth, your deep inner knowing. If you've been taking on too much to your own detriment, this is the time to let that go. If you've been saying yes one too many times, not setting clear boundaries around your time and energy and worth or giving away your power, this moon will help you to give yourself the love, care and attention you need to bring yourself back into balance.

You'll also find this moon shines a light on relationships with others, whether in a romantic sense or with family, friends and colleagues. This is a wonderful moon to heal and release any old relationship wounds and find forgiveness. A true mediator, Libra will help you to find peace and harmony in relationships that may have been fraught and see the other sides of situations. This moon will also help you to see any relationships you are holding on to that are creating upset and instability, so that you can either set clearer boundaries or finally let go of them with grace and love.

☾ The Libra full-moon soul reflections

In what areas of your life do you most feel a lack of equilibrium?

....

....

....

....

....

....

....

Where are you most trying to hold on to or control things in your life, desperately trying to make things work or fit the way you feel they need to be?

....

....

....

....

....

....

....

Where have you been giving away too much of yourself and not leaving enough for you? What boundaries do you need to put in place around your own self-care? Perhaps diarise time for this – time for you – like you would with other people. Make this non-negotiable and value it, whether it's an undisturbed 15 minutes every morning, or a once-a-week spa appointment or an evening off every few weeks.

....

....

....

....

....

....

....

Take a look at your past relationships and notice whether you still carry around any stories or hurts from these. Can you find forgiveness and move on?

....

....

....

....

....

....

....

Do a relationship review. What changes, if any, need to be made in the most important relationships in your life? Are you putting your time and effort in the right places? Are there any relationships that you need to let go of or move away from?

....

....

....

....

....

....

....

MY INSIGHTS, FEELINGS, GUIDANCE AND WISDOM FROM THE LIBRA FULL MOON

....

....

....

....

....

....

....

☾ On this Libra full moon, I am celebrating:

....

....

....

....

....

....

....

☾ Under the Libra full moon, I am releasing:

1..

....

2..

....

3..

....

☾ The waning-moon phase

Three actions I will take under the waning moon to help me release these things:

1..

....

2..

....

3..

....

☾ Last-quarter-moon check-in

What have you learned and experienced so far through the lunar cycle?

....

....

....

....

....

....

....

What are you ready to heal and release?

....

....

....

....

....

....

....

Scorpio Full Moon

Focus on transforming your life, stepping into
your power and following your desires.

Falls in Taurus season, between 20 April and 20 May
Ruled by Pluto
Fixed Water sign
Symbol: the Scorpion

You'll find the date of the next Scorpio full moon on my website: kirstygallagher.com

Date of Scorpio full moon ....

The Scorpio full moon comes along to propel you into awakening, truth and transformation. Under the illuminating light of this full moon, truths will begin to be revealed, power reclaimed and life mysteries solved.

Scorpio is a mysterious and mystical sign that's all about personal strength and recognising your inner wisdom and potential – your own magic and all that you are capable of.

Scorpio craves transformation in order to keep evolving, learning and growing, and so this moon will highlight for you where you are stuck in or obsessing over the past (especially if you feel you have been mistreated or wronged) or being kept down by any kind of negativity, insecurities, grudges, jealousies or resentments. It is a moon of seeking out the usually avoided, gritty truth, taking you right into your emotional depths.

Desire is a big trait of Scorpio, making this a moon that will help you to see where you put your desires on hold – or perhaps even where they scare you, preventing you from going after what you truly want in life. As one of the most intuitive signs of the zodiac, Scorpio will help you to tune into your deep inner knowing to awaken your inner power and yearnings and the truth about who you really are and what you really want from your life.

This is a potent moon for releasing and letting go of the doubts, the fears, the stories you tell yourself and the ways in which you stay small – anything and everything that's holding you back from shining your light, being your most authentic self and stepping into your power.

☾ The Scorpio full-moon soul reflections

Are there any parts of your past that you stay stuck in, or any hurts or resentments that you are still holding on to?

....

....

....

....

....

....

....

What emotions always tend to hold you back? Do you often feel insecure, afraid, unsure about certain areas of your life?

....

....

....

....

....

....

....

What desires do you have that you always put on hold and why?

....

....

....

....

....

....

....

What do you need to release from your life under this moon? Is it the past, limiting self-beliefs, stories you keep telling yourself?

....

....

....

....

....

....

....

This full moon reminds you of your power: how can you step more fully into it? Are there any areas where you need to take back that power and stand up for yourself, believing in all you are capable of?

....

....

....

....

....

....

....

MY INSIGHTS, FEELINGS, GUIDANCE AND WISDOM FROM THE SCORPIO FULL MOON

....

....

....

....

....

....

....

☾ **On this Scorpio full moon, I am celebrating:**

....

....

....

....

....

....

....

☾ **Under the Scorpio full moon, I am releasing:**

1..

....

2..

....

3..

....

☾ The waning-moon phase

Three actions I will take under the waning moon to help me release these things:

1..

....

2..

....

3..

....

☾ Last-quarter-moon check-in

What have you learned and experienced so far through the lunar cycle?

....

....

....

....

....

....

....

What are you ready to heal and release?

....

....

....

....

....

....

....

Sagittarius Full Moon

Focus on releasing all that keeps you from freedom, purpose and meaning in your life.

Falls in Gemini season, between 21 May and 20 June
Ruled by Jupiter
Mutable Fire sign
Symbol: the Archer

You'll find the date of the next Sagittarius full moon on my website: kirstygallagher.com

Date of Sagittarius full moon ....

The adventurer of the zodiac, the Sagittarius full moon is here to help you find freedom and meaning in your life and encourage you to follow your heart and your inner wisdom.

This is a moon of truth, and as this full moon shines her light, it will become obvious to you where, who and what restricts your freedom, curbing your adventure and passion for life. This is a moon that will show you all of the restraints, constraints and limitations (both external and internal) that are keeping you from living life to the full. If you're stuck in a job or relationship that's not for you, for example, holding yourself back by playing small or stagnant or stuck in any areas of your life, it will be too obvious to ignore.

This full moon will highlight all the areas in which you can't speak your truth or show up as your most authentic self. It will also flag where, out of fear, you ignore your inner wisdom, the direction your heart wants you to go in or the opportunities that life offers you. It will show you where you focus too much on the negative and what could go wrong, rather than taking a risk and trusting that it could, in fact, all go right!

As the last full moon before the summer solstice, this moon wants you to release all of this so you can adventure into summer and grab opportunities as they come along. This is a moon that helps you to seek the meaning of your life, and actually life in general, opening yourself up to all that's possible for you when you get into alignment with your heart and begin to live life as though you're on purpose.

☾ The Sagittarius full-moon soul reflections

Where in your life do you feel most stagnant, stuck or restricted?

....

....

....

....

....

....

....

Where do you feel you can't show up as your most authentic self, speak up and say what you really mean? In what situations do you feel you need to hide parts – or all – of who you are?

....

....

....

....

....

....

....

In what ways do you focus too much on what could go wrong, rather than believing it could work out perfectly?

....

....

....

....

....

....

....

What do you need to release from your life so that you can adventure into summer and say yes to all opportunities that come your way?

....

....

....

....

....

....

....

Take a moment to imagine that your entire life was on purpose. How does that feel? What would you do differently if you trusted in the purpose of it all?

....

....

....

....

....

....

....

MY INSIGHTS, FEELINGS, GUIDANCE AND WISDOM FROM THE SAGITTARIUS FULL MOON

....

....

....

....

....

....

....

☾ On this Sagittarius full moon, I am celebrating:

....

....

....

....

....

....

....

☾ Under the Sagittarius full moon, I am releasing:

1..

....

2..

....

3..

....

☾ The waning-moon phase

Three actions I will take under the waning moon to help me release these things:

1..

....

2..

....

3..

....

☾ Last-quarter-moon check-in

What have you learned and experienced so far through the lunar cycle?

....

....

....

....

....

....

....

What are you ready to heal and release?

....

....

....

....

....

....

....

Capricorn Full Moon

*Focus on chasing your dreams, building a firm
life foundation and becoming more trusting.*

Falls in Cancer season, between 21 June and 22 July
Ruled by Saturn
Cardinal Earth sign
Symbol: the Goat

You'll find the date of the next Capricorn full moon on my
website: kirstygallagher.com

Date of Capricorn full moon ....

The first full moon after the summer solstice, this one comes
along to help you shift anything that is not in alignment with
your life for the second half of the traditional year.

Ambitious, hardworking, dedicated and persistent, the
Capricorn full moon lights up a drive within you to achieve
all of your goals and aspirations. If you have been giving your
dreams enough attention, this moon will feel inspiring and

bring an ambitious motivation like never before; if you've been avoiding going after what you want, however, you'll feel its intensity as it highlights and shakes up whatever is standing in the way.

This moon brings a great opportunity to notice where you resist change: to break things down and up, so that they can be rebuilt on firm foundations. Rather than continually tiptoeing along in a relationship that's going nowhere, a career path that doesn't fulfil you, having a sense of self and/or beliefs that can be shattered at the first sign of doubt, this moon wants for you only what is real and true and lasting.

This moon is about restructuring, and as the foundations of your life are shaken, this is a wonderful chance to get to know yourself and your direction in life: what is real for you? What do you believe in? What are your values? Who do you want to be? How do you want to show up in the world? And what do you want from life? These are all questions you need to be asking under this illuminating full moon.

One last important note for this moon: notice what you are trying to grip and cling to and control. As mentioned, the Capricorn moon shows you where you have real resistance to change – in particular, letting go of control. Notice where you do this in your life and invite in more trust.

☾ The Capricorn full-moon soul reflections

Have you been giving your dreams the necessary attention?
If not, why not? What have you been avoiding?

....

....

....

....

....

....

....

Lay some firm foundations for yourself – how can you support
and believe in yourself more? Who and what can you rely
on?

....

....

....

....

....

....

....

What is shifting and changing in your life right now? Does your relationship feel rocky? Are you uncertain about your career path, or are your beliefs and values being tested?

....

....

....

....

....

....

....

What direction would you like your life to take in this second half of the year? What would you like to achieve?

....

....

....

....

....

....

....

What do you most try and control and hold on to in your life?
Can you invite in more trust around these areas?

....

....

....

....

....

....

....

MY INSIGHTS, FEELINGS, GUIDANCE AND
WISDOM FROM THE CAPRICORN FULL MOON

....

....

....

....

....

....

....

☾ **On this Capricorn full moon, I am celebrating:**

....

....

....

....

....

....

....

☾ **Under the Capricorn full moon, I am releasing:**

1..

..:..

2..

....

3..

....

☾ The waning-moon phase

Three actions I will take under the waning moon to help me release these things:

1..

....

2..

....

3..

....

☾ Last-quarter-moon check-in

What have you learned and experienced so far through the lunar cycle?

....

....

....

....

....

....

....

....

What are you ready to heal and release?

....

....

....

....

....

....

....

Aquarius Full Moon

*Focus on releasing what limits and holds
you back, trusting in your journey and
becoming your most authentic self.*

Falls in Leo season, between 23 July and 22 August
Ruled by Saturn and Uranus
Fixed Air sign
Symbol: the Water Bearer

You'll find the date of the next Aquarius full moon on my
website: kirstygallagher.com

Date of Aquarius full moon ....

The Aquarius full moon comes along to illuminate the skies
and your need for the freedom to be yourself. There may be a
real feeling of things shifting around this full moon, a sense
of a stirring energy in the pit of your belly, and you might find
yourself prowling, pacing up and down and feeling restless
and restricted, as this moon calls you to break free.

You will be able to see and feel so clearly all the areas in your life where you are stuck – bound not just by external factors but also by yourself. You will feel as though you are fed up with being held down and held back and the need for freedom will be strong. You'll realise how exhausted you are from pretending to be someone or something you're not and/or doing and saying the things expected of you for so long.

This moon can have quite an emotionally detached quality to it, which makes it good for letting go of emotional attachments and anything that has been restricting you. This will help you to break out of patterns of behaviours that no longer serve, and to release all that's not meant for you, once and for all.

This moon is here to help you to fearlessly seek your truth and, most of all, to find an unwavering faith in where your journey is taking you. Trust that your soul knows best and that when you let things fall away, you will be left with the most authentic version of yourself and what is lasting and true for you. This is the greatest freedom.

☾ The Aquarius full-moon soul reflections

Where do you feel most stuck and held back, or as though you are always trying to live up to other people's or society's expectations?

....

....

....

....

....

....

....

What patterns do you tend to repeat in your life over and over again?

....

....

....

....

....

....

....

How do you always hold yourself back? What restrictions, limiting beliefs or unrealistic expectations do you put on yourself?

....

....

....

....

....

....

....

What do you need to allow to fall away from your life under this full moon?

....

....

....

....

....

....

....

Who would you be if you were completely free to be yourself? How would your life be different?

....

....

....

....

....

....

....

MY INSIGHTS, FEELINGS, GUIDANCE AND WISDOM FROM THE AQUARIUS FULL MOON

....

....

....

....

....

....

....

🌙 **On this Aquarius full moon, I am celebrating:**

....

....

....

....

....

....

....

🌙 **Under the Aquarius full moon, I am releasing:**

1...

....

2...

....

3...

....

☾ The waning-moon phase

Three actions I will take under the waning moon to help me release these things:

1...

....

2...

....

3...

....

☾ Last-quarter-moon check-in

What have you learned and experienced so far through the lunar cycle?

....

....

....

....

....

....

....

What are you ready to heal and release?

....

....

....

....

....

....

....

Pisces Full Moon

Focus on closure and completion, an emotional cleansing and awakening to your soul connection.

Falls in Virgo season, between 23 August and 22 September
Ruled by Neptune and Jupiter
Mutable Water sign
Symbol: the Fish

You'll find the date of the next Pisces full moon on my website: kirstygallagher.com

Date of Pisces full moon ....

The last sign of the zodiac, and last full moon before we turn seasons and move into autumn, this full moon truly is a time of culmination, closure, completion and a deep emotional cleanse. This full moon is here to help you close off a life chapter, so that you can step into something new.

As one of the most spiritual signs of the zodiac, Pisces wants to help awaken your connection to your soul and your path in life – to help you get back in touch with your dreams, intuition and inner-guidance system and once again flow with life and find the everyday magic.

But first you need to realise all that stands in the way of that. And so this full moon will take you into deep healing, as the gentle waters of Pisces help to soothe, cleanse and renew your emotions, bringing deep insights, awakenings, growth and answers.

Due to this, there will be an air of emotional sensitivity and vulnerability around this moon – a sense of wanting to blame anyone and everything for the way your life is, or feeling like the victim or martyr and/or wanting to avoid or escape it all. This happens to help show you where in your life you have been giving your power away, not creating clear boundaries (a huge Pisces lesson) – but especially where you have been ignoring your own intuition, inner niggles and perhaps turning away from the call of your own soul to meet other people's dreams, needs and desires.

This Pisces full moon will help you to see what has to be released, forgiven, unravelled, completed and what you need to step away from and not take into the next season with you.

☾ The Pisces full-moon soul reflections

What emotions is this moon bringing to the surface and what are they showing you? Is there a sense of any blame or being a victim or wanting to avoid certain things?

....

....

....

....

....

....

....

Who and what do you need to forgive, so that you can move forward and leave the past behind?

....

....

....

....

....

....

....

How connected do you feel to your intuition, and following signs that you get? How can you turn more inward over this moon? Maybe through daily meditation, moments of quiet contemplation or checking in with yourself before making big decisions?

....

....

....

....

....

....

....

Which chapters in your life need to come to an end? What has not been working for a while that you need to complete or close?

....

....

....

....

....

....

....

Where do you put others' feelings and needs before your own? How can you begin to put yourself and your desires first a bit more? This may mean clearer boundaries around the amount of time and energy you give to others, and saying no every now and then.

....

....

....

....

....

....

....

MY INSIGHTS, FEELINGS, GUIDANCE AND WISDOM FROM THE PISCES FULL MOON

....

....

....

....

....

....

....

☽ On this Pisces full moon, I am celebrating:

....

....

....

....

....

....

....

☽ Under the Pisces full moon, I am releasing:

1..

....

2..

....

3..

....

☾ The waning-moon phase

Three actions I will take under the waning moon to help me release these things:

1...
....

2...
....

3...
....

☾ Last-quarter-moon check-in

What have you learned and experienced so far through the lunar cycle?

....
....
....
....
....
....
....

What are you ready to heal and release?

....

....

....

....

....

....

....

CHAPTER 6

The 13th Moon

As a 'lunar year' is only 354 days (as opposed to our calendar year of 365 days), this means that in most years there will be 25 moons in a calendar year: 12 new and 13 full (or vice versa). Use this section for the 13th moon and allow your intuition and what you have learned on your lunar journey so far to guide you. Tune into this moon for yourself: what do you feel it is trying to show or teach you?

Date of the moon ....

Zodiac sign the moon falls in ....

- 224 -

☾ The 13th-moon soul reflections

What emotions have you been experiencing in the run-up to this moon, and what have they been showing you?

....

....

....

....

....

....

....

How would you describe the energies of this moon – motivating, grounding, inspiring, heavy, emotional, unsettling? And how is it making you feel?

....

....

....

....

....

....

....

What areas of your life are coming under the moonlight with this moon? What do you think this moon is asking you to look at?

....

....

....

....

....

....

Can you identify one action or change you are being called to make under this moon?

....

....

....

....

....

....

....

What do you feel this moon is trying to show or teach you? What wisdom is this moon offering you? If the moon could talk to you what would she say?

....

....

....

....

....

....

....

MY INSIGHTS, FEELINGS, GUIDANCE AND WISDOM FROM THE 13TH MOON

....

....

....

....

....

....

....

If the moon is a NEW MOON:

☾ My 13th new-moon intentions are:

1...

....

2...

....

3...

....

☾ The waxing-moon phase

Three actions I will take during the waxing moon to help take me closer to my new-moon intentions:

1...

....

2...

....

3...

....

☾ First-quarter-moon check-in

What seems to be falling into place or coming together, taking you closer to your new-moon intentions?

....

....

....

....

....

....

What seems to be difficult or challenging, and are any doubts and fears surfacing?

....

....

....

....

....

....

....

If the moon is a FULL MOON:

☾ On this 13th full moon, I am celebrating:

....

....

....

....

....

....

....

☾ Under the 13th full moon, I am releasing:

1..

....

2..

....

3..

....

☾ The waning-moon phase

Three actions I will take under the waning moon to help me release these things:

1..

....

2..

....

3..

....

☾ Last-quarter-moon check-in

What have you learned and experienced so far through the lunar cycle?

....

....

....

....

....

....

....

What are you ready to heal and release?

....

....

....

....

....

....

....

Final Thoughts

WELL DONE – you did it! A full year of Lunar Living and moon magic. I trust that it has been insightful, enlightening and life changing for you. I am so incredibly proud of you for dedicating this time to yourself and your own growth, committing to moving in the direction of your dreams. My greatest wish is that you have developed a knowing, belief and trust in yourself, and that you can see, without doubt, that you are guided by a great wisdom in the sky. As my wonderful friend Ash Radford sings in his song 'Guided By Waves':

*'Trust in the moon, she whispers
we'll be there soon.'*

I truly hope the moon has helped you to find your way this year. Now let's celebrate you. Looking back since you first started this journal a year ago:

How has your life most changed over the last year?

....

....

....

What has been your greatest life adjustment or achievement? What are you most proud of yourself for?

....

....

....

What was difficult? What challenged you?

....

....

....

What did you learn and how did you grow through these challenges? Can you see the blessing in the burden?

....

....

....

....

....

What have you discovered about yourself and life? What are three of your greatest lessons?

....

....

....

....

....

....

....

....

....

....

I always love to hear from you, so please do share your thoughts with me on Instagram, tagging me @kirsty_gallagher_ so that we can celebrate you and share this captivating way of living by the moon.

And don't forget – you can read in more detail about the sign the moon is in either in *Lunar Living: Working With the Magic of the Moon Cycles* or by signing up for my Lunar Love Notes on my website: www.kirstygallagher.com.

Acknowledgements

To my wonderful family: Sandra, Kylie, Kerry, Liam, Stephanie, Soraya, Jake, Chloe, Edward, Isaac and my late Grandpa Donald. I love you all and thank you for always loving and supporting me.

My editor, Holly Whitaker, thank you for being the best and for your continual support and encouragement; I love creating books with you! And to all the wonderful people at Yellow Kite who have supported me on this journey, thank you. I am so grateful to Myrto Kalavrezou and Caitriona Horne for your PR and marketing skills, Anne Newman for your editing magic and Jo Myler for creating the book cover of dreams. Thank you to The Colour Study for your wonderful illustrations.

If you are holding this journal in your hands, thank you for allowing me to share my passion for *Lunar Living* with you. I hope it changes your life as much as it has mine. I always love to hear from you so please do share your moon magic with me.

My Lunar Living online sisterhood, thank you for all your support, lunar love and for being the best sisterhood ever. My never-ending gratitude to my right-hand woman Helen Elias, *Lunar Living* would not be what it is without you.

To all of you who have attended my online yoga, moon, meditation workshops, 'Still Space' meditations on Instagram, thank you for being part of this magical community and continuing to show up for yourself and each other. Remember, you are never alone, you've got this, I've got you, we've got each other.

Thank you to my sisterhood: Becki Rabin, Megan Rose Lane, Wendy O'Beirne, Samantha Day, Caggie Dunlop, Hannah Holt, Seema Sopal, Claire Williams, Lisa Strong, Rebecca Dennis and Adele Hartshorn. And to Ian Steed and James Lee Dawkins for being you.

To everyone who has allowed me to offer you guidance on your life journey through my soul guidance readings and coaching/mentoring, thank you for your willingness to trust me with your heart and soul. I love seeing you show up in the world.

To all my students and anyone who has ever attended a class, course, retreat or workshop with me, thank you for trusting me with your body, mind, heart and soul. I appreciate you more than you know. And thank you to all my current private and corporate clients for bearing with me through this writing journey, your support and kindness has been invaluable. To Harbottle and Lewis, iZettle, Selfridges, Fitbit, Women's Health Live and my lululemon family, thank you for your support.

If I have not named you it's not because you are forgotten or that I am not grateful. It's simply that I have been blessed to have so many wonderful people touch my life and not enough pages left to mention you all, it would be another book in itself! If you have ever been a part of my life in any way, thank you.

Finally, my biggest thanks to the Moon, as without her wisdom, support, guidance and ebb and flow, none of this would be possible.

About the Author

Photograph by Jen Armstrong

Kirsty Gallagher is a moon mentor, soul alignment and transformation coach, yoga teacher, meditation teacher and *Sunday Times* bestselling author with an infectious passion for life.

She has been sharing the life-changing benefits of yoga and the moon for 13 years through classes, workshops, private and corporate sessions, and has taught over 80 worldwide retreats. She is the founder of the online sisterhood *Lunar Living*, which teaches you how to weave the secret and ancient wisdom of the moon into modern, everyday life.

Kirsty works alongside women helping them live back in alignment with an ancient cycle, a natural rhythm and flow, and she helps them to connect back into their authenticity and purpose. Weaving lunar wisdom with soul guidance readings, astrology and cutting-edge transformational coaching techniques, Kirsty helps women to overcome doubts, fears and self-sabotage to find a deep inner connection and meaning in life.

Kirsty has shared moon magic on The Chris Evans Breakfast Show and *This Morning* and been featured in *YOU Magazine, Stylist, Red Magazine, Women's Health, Soul and Spirit Magazine* and *Natural Health Magazine*.

Described as down to earth, warm-hearted, compassionate and inspiring, Kirsty is known for bringing ancient mystical practices and wisdom to modern day life in a relatable way that anyone and everyone can take something from. Find out more at www.kirstygallagher.com.